BULLETIN OF THE JOHN RYLANDS LIBRARY

VOLUME 101 NUMBER 1, SPRING 2025

BULLETIN OF THE JOHN RYLANDS LIBRARY

ISSN 2054-9318 (Print)
ISSN 2054-9326 (Online)
ISBN 9781526194565

Established in 1903

Published by Manchester University Press and the University of Manchester Library
Manchester University Press, 176 Waterloo Place, Manchester, M13 9GP, UK
Email: mup@manchester.ac.uk
Web address: www.manchesteruniversitypress.co.uk

University of Manchester Library, Oxford Road, Manchester, M13 9PP, UK
Tel: +44 (0)161 275 3751
Web address: www.library.manchester.ac.uk

The publication of the *Bulletin of the John Rylands Library* is made possible by funding from The University of Manchester Library.

Members of the Editorial Board 2025

Chair: David Matthews
Editors: Fred Schurink, Rachel Winchcombe and Huw Twiston Davies
Editorial Assistant: Emma Nelson

Editorial Board
Guyda Armstrong
Paul Fouracre
Roy Gibson
David Law
Phyllis Mack
Janette Martin
John Morgan
Walter Pohl
Lynda Pratt
Ingrid Rembold
Carsten Timmermann
Huw Twiston Davies
Jack Webb

Subscriptions

An electronic version of this issue is available to read online under a CC BY-NC-ND licence, at
https://www.manchesterhive.com/view/journals/bjrl/bjrl-overview.xml

Print editions for issues 96.2 and onwards are available to purchase at
https://manchesteruniversitypress.co.uk

EU authorised representative for GPSR:
Easy Access System Europe, Mustamäe tee 50, 10621 Tallinn, Estonia
gpsr.requests@easproject.com

BULLETIN OF THE JOHN RYLANDS LIBRARY

VOLUME 101 NUMBER 1 SPRING 2025

CONTENTS

Editorial Fred Schurink and Huw Twiston Davies	1

Articles

A New Edition of Eleven Fragmentary Neo-Sumerian Texts in the John Rylands Library, University of Manchester Changyu Liu and Qier Zhang	3
University of Manchester Library 23025: A Single-Leaf Print of the Crucifixion from a Late Medieval Etched Metal Plate, or a Nineteenth-Century Forgery? Edward Potten	17
Adaption and Experimentation: The Evolution of Charles Calvert's Acting Edition of *The Tempest* Ian Martin Nickson	39
Religious Revival and the Challenge of Evangelical Primitivism: Opposition to the Brethren and Lay Preachers in Ulster after the 1859 Revival Andrew R. Holmes	61
'Rex Dei Gratia': Mark Hovell's Forgotten Essay on *The Divine Right of Kings* Chris Godden	83

Editorial

The *Bulletin of the John Rylands Library* was founded in 1903, a mere three years after the Library opened its doors to the public on 1 January 1900. While the founding editors had lofty ambitions for the *Bulletin* to 'not only promote the use of books [in the John Rylands Library], but directly tend to the advancement of knowledge', they described its 'real purpose' as 'the list of accessions'.[1] Over the decades, that remit gradually broadened, particularly following the incorporation of the Library into The University of Manchester in 1972. The journal took on its current form after Manchester University Press took over the production of the *Bulletin* in 2013, resuming its core mission to showcase and shed light on the Special Collections of the John Rylands Library in order to expand our knowledge and understanding of the cultures in which they were produced and consumed.[2]

When the Press took charge of the publication of the *Bulletin*, it also improved access by publishing new and past issues online. As the *Bulletin* moves into its second century of volumes, we are delighted to announce that Manchester University Press has agreed to publish the journal Open Access from the present issue, advancing the journal's mission to bring scholarship that complements the Library's collections to the widest possible audience. Publication will be on a diamond Open Access model, funded by the University of Manchester Library, with no requirement for article processing charges. The transition reflects the commitment of the Press, the Library and the University as well as the *Bulletin*'s editorial team to Open Research, enhancing the reach and accessibility of the journal and its impact on society.[3] Contributors can look forward to a wider readership, a larger number of citations and a greater social impact, while the journal will continue to offer the same quality control (including double-blind peer review) and editorial services.

As well as moving to Open Access, the *Bulletin* has also expanded its remit to reflect both the development of the Library's collections and the cutting-edge scholarly approaches to the collections spearheaded by academic and library staff associated with the John Rylands Research Institute and Library (JRRIL). The new editorial team (Co-editors Fred Schurink and Rachel Winchcombe and acting co-editor Huw Twiston Davies) particularly welcome contributions on the Library's less well known modern, contemporary and non-European collections. It is a pleasure to include a study of the ancient Neo-Sumerian Texts in the JRRIL in this issue, while the previous issue, *Higher Learning and Civic Cultures of Knowledge: Manchester 1824–2024* (100.1), contained contributions drawing on the less-explored twentieth-century University Archives. The forthcoming special issue on *Imaging Heritage Science Initiatives at The John Rylands Research Institute and Library, University of Manchester* (101.2), in turn, will include articles on the Sri Guru Granth Sahib (Punjabi MS 5), the Gaster Jewish Amulets and early modern New World featherwork. We are also in discussion about projects on the Library's Humanitarian Archive and the email correspondence in the Carcanet Press Archive, and we are equally keen to publish scholarship on the Library's outstanding Arabic, Persian, Turkish and South-East Asian manuscript collections, among others.

The second major area in which we want to encourage contributions is digital and scientific approaches to the study of manuscripts, printed books and other materials in library and heritage collections. The JRRIL has been at the forefront of this field through the partnership it has fostered between library professionals, technical and IT staff, and academics. This will be reflected in the next issue of the *Bulletin*, which will include studies on the application of a range of imaging techniques (from Raman spectroscopy and multispectral imaging to 3D photogrammetry) to a variety of materials, as well as historical and social and cultural reflections on this work. At the same time, the editorial team remains committed to the publication of scholarship in established areas of specialisation of the Library. In the present issue, the article 'Religious Revival and the Challenge of Evangelical Primitivism: Opposition to the Brethren and Lay Preachers in Ulster after the 1859 Revival' reflects the global significance of the Library's holdings in non-conformist religious history, which recently received another major boost by the addition of Dr Williams's Library to the collections.[4]

The founding editors expressed the hope and expectation that the *Bulletin* would 'from time to time to deal with much that concerns bibliography ..., us[ing] the term in its broadest sense, as the science of books considered under all aspects'.[5] We remain committed to publishing excellent research that draws on books in all their forms, particularly from, or related to, the collections of the JRRIL, as a window onto our shared past. We welcome contributions that apply new technologies and perspectives to manuscripts and printed books and shed light on recent or overlooked parts of the collections of the JRRIL, while continuing to provide a trusted venue for scholarship of the highest quality related to traditional areas of strength of the collections.

Fred Schurink
Huw Twiston Davies

Notes

1 'Introductory Note', *Bulletin of the John Rylands Library*, 1 (1903–08), 1–3 (p. 1).
2 Paul Fouracre and Sasha Handley, 'Editorial', *Bulletin of the John Rylands Library*, 91 (2015), 5–6.
3 www.openresearch.manchester.ac.uk/.
4 https://dwl.ac.uk/.
5 'Introductory Note', p. 1.

A New Edition of Eleven Fragmentary Neo-Sumerian Texts in the John Rylands Library, University of Manchester

CHANGYU LIU, SHANDONG UNIVERSITY
QIER ZHANG, ZHEJIANG NORMAL UNIVERSITY

Abstract
The eleven unpublished Ur III cuneiform texts presented in this article are housed in the John Rylands Library, University of Manchester. This article publishes two tablets from Puzrish-Dagan which deal with dead animals; six from Umma involving various contents; one from Girsu on the receipt of barley; one from Irisagrig with unclear recording; and one tablet with unknown provenience. Except for one text (no. 8), most are undated because of the damaged and fragmental preservation.

Keywords: cuneiform tablets; Neo-Sumerian; Puzrish-Dagan; Umma; Ur III Dynasty

The Third Dynasty of Ur (2112–2004 BC, i.e. the Ur III Dynasty, or Ur III for short) was a comparatively short but significant dynasty in ancient Mesopotamian civilisation, dating to the late third millennium BC, preceded by the Early Dynastic (Old Sumerian) and Akkadian periods as well as the Gutian interregnum. Since the dynasty is said in the Sumerian King List to be the third from Ur to rule over Sumer, the period has been called the Third Dynasty of Ur (also called the Neo-Sumerian period), which comprises the reigns of five kings, namely Ur-Nammu (18 years), Shulgi (48 years), Amar-Suen (9 years), Shu-Suen (9 years) and Ibbi-Suen (24 or 25 years). During the reign of Ur-Nammu and the first half reign of his successor Shulgi, rulers devoted themselves to the unity of the Sumerian city-states and the conquest of the Akkadian areas. Subsequently, during his second half reign, Shulgi subdued neighbouring areas and extended his territory to the east and northeast by means of political alliances and military raids. In the reign of Amar-Suen, its third ruler, the dynasty flourished and reached its peak, with many thousands of administrative records but few military achievements. From the reign of Shu-Suen to that of Ibbi-Suen, the dynasty gradually weakened, collapsed, and was finally ended by the conquest of the Elamites. Following the collapse of the Ur III Dynasty, the periods of the Babylonian and Assyrian civilisations followed during the second and first millennia BC. The Ur III Dynasty was a highly centralised bureaucratic state. Its territory stretched east into Iran, and north towards the edge of northeastern Syria, northern Iraq and northwestern Iran, and consisted of three sections: the core, the periphery and the vassal states.[1]

The Third Dynasty of Ur is considered to be the best-documented period in the ancient Near East. So far, at least 100,000 cuneiform clay tablets dating to this period have been (legally and illegally) unearthed from the southern Iraq, mainly from seven sites: Umma (modern Tell Jokha), Girsu (modern Tell Telloh), Puzrish-Dagan (modern Drehem), Ur (modern Tell el-Muqayyar), Nippur (modern Nuffar), Irisagrig (modern site unclear) and Garshana (modern site unclear).[2] Cataloguing and publishing cuneiform texts is fundamental and indispensable for the reconstruction of the administration and daily life of the Ur III Dynasty, and the editing of unpublished cuneiform texts is always crucial to this task.

As one of the largest cuneiform collections in the United Kingdom, the John Rylands Library in University of Manchester houses at least 1,019 cuneiform tablets and fragments dating to the Ur III period, the overwhelming majority of which have been published by numerous scholars since the early twentieth century.[3] In 1915, Charles Bedale published fifty-eight cuneiform texts (JRL Bedale 01 ~ 58).[4] Three of these texts were re-edited by Samuel Mercer in 1928 (JRL Bedale 35) and 1929 (JRL Bedale 37 and 47).[5] In 1932, Thomas Fish published as many as 839 Ur III texts (JRL 0024, 0028–0659, 0659a, 0670–0769, and 0780–0884), and re-edited JRL Bedale 01–58.[6] Of these, twenty-six texts had previously been published by Fish in 1924 (JRL 0166, 0207, 0254, 0256, 0293, 0393, 0878, 0879 and 0884), 1925 (JRL 0263), 1927 (JRL 0218, 0221 and 0487), 1928 (JRL 0220) and 1929 (JRL 0057–0059, 0065–0069 and 0081–0082); and nine texts were later re-edited by Edmond Sollberger in 1966 (JRL 0530–0532), by Tohru Gomi in 1982 (JRL 0880–0883), and Claus Wilcke in 1999 (JRL 0527 and 0630).[7] In 1962, Trevor Donald published one text (JRL 0930).[8] In 1981–82, Gomi published eighty-six texts (JRL 0932–1007 and 1009–1018).[9] In 2000, Farouk al-Rawi published thirty-one texts (JRL 1019, 1021–1025, 1027–1030, 1032–1035, 1038–1040, 1076–1084, 1086–1087, 1088a, 1088b and 1088c).[10]

This article provides a new edition of eleven fragmental and illegible cuneiform tablets kept in the John Rylands Library, which consist of four unpublished texts (JRL 1008, 1088d, 1088e and 1088f) and seven previously catalogued texts (JRL 1025, 1028, 1029, 1030, 1032, 1033 and 1035). Their photographs are available at the Cuneiform Digital Library Initiative (CDLI). There, one text (JRL 1028) has been transliterated by Robert K. Englund.

In this article, based on the photographs provided by CDLI and Database of Neo-Sumerian Texts (BDTNS), the authors (re-)transliterate, translate and comment on these texts, the essential details of which may be found in Table 1.

No. 1 – Receipt of barley

Shelfmark: JRL 1008
Provenience: Girsu
Date: – viii

Table 1
Cuneiform texts in the John Rylands Library

No.	Shelfmark	Provenience	Date	Sealing	CDLI	BDTNS
1	JRL 1008	Girsu	– viii	yes	P430841	211187
2	JRL 1025	Umma	– – –	no	P430846	187686
3	JRL 1028	Puzrish-Dagan	– – 4+	no	P332651	047665
4	JRL 1029	Umma	– – –	no	P332652	047666
5	JRL 1030	Umma	– – –	no	P332653	047667
6	JRL 1032	Puzrish-Dagan	(AS 3) v 2	no	P332654	047668
7	JRL 1033	Umma?	– iv 10	no	P332655	047669
8	JRL 1035	Umma	SS 1 iii	no	P332656	047670
9	JRL 1088d	Irisagrig	– – –	no	P430886	–
10	JRL 1088e	uncertain	– – –	yes	P430887	–
11	JRL 1088f	Umma?	– – –	no	P430888	–

Text

obv.

    1) 10-la$_2$-1 še [gur lugal]   *9 royal gur barley*
    2) ki Ad-da-ta   *from Adda,*

rev.

    1) Lu$_2$-du$_{10}$-ga/šu ba-ti   *Lu-duga received.*
    2) iti ezem ^{d}Ba-ba$_6$ *Month: 'Festival of Baba.'*

seal

    1) Lu$_2$-du$_{10}$-[ga]   *Lu-duga*
    2) dub-[sar]   *scribe*
    3) dumu KA-[KA]   *son of KA-KA.*

Introduction

This text is the envelope of the tablet *BJRL* 64, 098 01, which records a transfer of barley from Adda to Lu-duga. For the abbreviatory publication, see the online database Cuneiform Digital Library Initiative (https://cdli.mpiwg-berlin.mpg.de/), *sic passim*. The same transfer also occurred in Umma texts with the same seal inscription.

Commentary

For the receipt of barley from Adda to Lu-duga in Umma archives, see *BJRL* 64, 104 36; *AAICAB* 1/3, pl. 224, Bod S 185.

For the reconstruction of the sealing, cf. *Nisaba* 33, 567 (Umma); *AAICAB* 1/3, pl. 224, Bod S 185 (Umma).

No. 2 – Delivery of travel basket

Shelfmark: JRL 1025
Provenience: Umma
Date: ---
Catalogue: Iraq 62, 022 JRL 1025 catalogue

Text

obv

    1) 1 gi [...]   *1 ... reed ...*
    below destroyed

rev.

    1) [x] ^{gi}kaskal ku$_6$ nun gid$_2$ *x travel basket(s) putting long nun-fish,*
    2) [x] 10 ku$_6$ kun-zi-da   *10+ kun-zi-fish*
    3) Ur-^{d}Ba-ba$_6$ enku   *of Ur-Baba the tax-collector;*
    4) 2 ^{gi}kaskal ku$_6$ nun gid$_2$ *2 travel baskets putting long nun-fish,*
    5) 1 ^{gi}kaskal ku$_6$ kun-zi-da   *1 travel basket putting kun-zi-fish,*
    6) Ur-^{d}A-ba-ba   *of Ur-Ababa;*
    7) 2 ^{gi}kaskal ku$_6$ nun gid$_2$ *2 travel baskets putting long nun-fish,*
    8) Ur-^{d}Ma-mi   *of Ur-Mami;*
    9) mu-DU ša$_3$ Uri$_5$[^{ki}-ma]   *delivery at Ur.*

Introduction

The text records the delivery of various travel baskets by three individuals: Ur-Baba, Ur-Ababa and Ur-Mami.

Commentary

rev. 1) For the term ku$_6$ nun, see R. K. Englund, *Organisation und Verwaltung der Ur III-Fischerei* (Berlin: Dietrich Reimer Verlag, 1990), p. 215.

rev. 2) For the term ku$_6$ kun-zi(-da), 'teichgezüchtete Fische', see R. K. Englund, *Organisation und Verwaltung der Ur III-Fischerei* (Berlin: Dietrich Reimer Verlag, 1990), p. 209.

rev. 3) Cf. *YOS* 04, 003; *STA* 11. For the term enku, 'collector of tributes', see G. Visicato, *The Bureaucracy of Šuruppak: Administrative Centres, Central Offices, Intermediate Structures and Hierarchies in the Economic Documentation of Fara* (Münster: Ugarit-Verlag, 1995), pp. 131–3.

No. 3 – Receipt of dead animals

Shelfmark: JRL 1028
Provenience: Puzrish-Dagan
Date: --4+
Catalogue: Iraq 62, 022 JRL 1028 catalogue

Text

obv.

    beginning containing number and type of animals broken
    1') ba-[ug$_7$]   dead
    2') u$_4$ [n]+4-[kam]   on the 4th day,
    3') ki Šu-Er$_3$-ra-t[a]   from Shu-Erra,

rev.

    1) [PN]   someone
    2) [š]u b[a-t]i   received.
    3) [i]ti ezem-[...]   Month: 'Festival of ...'
    4) [mu ...]   Year: ...

Introduction

This text deals with the receipt of dead animals from Shu-Erra, an official in the Puzrish-Dagan organisation who dealt exclusively with equids (dusu$_2$) dating between Amar-Suen 2 and Amar-Suen 6. For the administration of Shu-Erra from Puzrish-Dagan archives, see C. Liu, *Organization, Administrative Practices and Written Documentation in Mesopotamia during the Ur III Period (c.2112–2004 BC): A Case Study of Puzriš-Dagan in the Reign of Amar-Suen* (Münster: Ugarit-Verlag, 2017), pp. 365–8.

Commentary

rev. 1) From the Puzrish-Dagan archives, it is speculated that the unnamed official who received the dead animals from Shu-Erra was either Ur-nigar (Šulgi 43 ~ Amar-Suen 3) or Shulgi-irimu (Amar-Suen 3 ~ Ibbi-Suen 2). For Ur-nigar and Shulgi-irimu from Puzrish-Dagan archives, see C. Tsouparopoulou, 'The Material Face of Bureaucracy: Writing, Sealing and Archiving Tablets for the Ur III State at Drehem' (PhD dissertation, University of Cambridge, 2008), pp. 249–59; C. Tsouparopoulou, 'Killing and Skinning Animals in the Ur III Period: The Puzriš-Dagan (Drehem) Office Managing of Dead Animals and Slaughter By-products', *Altorientalische Forschungen*, 40 (2013), 150–82.

No. 4 – About female workers

Shelfmark: JRL 1029
Provenience: Umma
Date: ---
Catalogue: Iraq 62, 022 JRL 1029 catalogue

Text

obv.

1) 100 [...] ge[me$_2$ (u$_4$ 1-še$_3$)] 100 [...] female workers (each for one day)
2) ugula Ur-[^{d}Šul]-/pa-UD.[DU] overseer: Ur-Shulpae;
3) 50 ugula [Ur]-^{d}Ma-[mi] 50 (female labourers, each for one day), overseer: Ur-Mami;
4) kišib Lugal-[e$_2$-mah]-/e under seal of Lugal-emah.

rev.

space blank

Introduction

This text records the management of female workers in Umma province. For the management of workers in Umma province, see P. Steinkeller, 'Corvée Labor in Ur III Times', in S. Garfinkle and M. Molina (eds), *From the 21st Century B.C. to the 21st Century A.D.: Proceedings of the International Conference on Sumerian Studies Held in Madrid 22-24 July 2010* (Winona Lake: Eisenbrauns, 2013), pp. 347–424; B. Studevent-Hickman, 'The Organization of Manual Labor in Ur III Babylonia' (PhD dissertation, Harvard University, 2006), pp. 22–100. For Ur III female workers, see B. Lafont, 'State employment of women during the Ur III period', *REFEMA*, 2013 (https://doi.org/10.58079/tja4, accessed 6 August 2024).

Commentary

obv. 2) For the reconstruction of this personal name, see *MVN* 18, 387.
obv. 3) For the reconstruction of this personal name, see *BPOA* 01, 0009; *BPOA* 01, 0010; *PPAC* 5, 1708.
obv. 4) For the reconstruction, see *SAT* 3, 2155.

No. 5 – Food allotment

Shelfmark: JRL 1030
Provenience: Umma
Date: ---
Catalogue: Iraq 62, 022 JRL 1030 catalogue

Text

obv.

beginning broken

1')	[...] KA	
2')	1 ku$_6$ sag-kur$_2$	1 beheaded fish
3')	1(aš) gu$_2$ šum$_2$ sikil	1 talent pure onion
4')	0.1.0 zu$_2$-lum	1 barig dates

rev.

1)	^{d}Nin-e$_2$-gal-igi-du	for Ninegal-igidu;
2)	10 ku$_6$ ^{gi}hal	10 baskets of fish
3)	1(aš) gu$_2$ šum$_2$ sikil	1 talent pure onion
4)	Lugal-[...]	for Lugal-[...];
5)	1 [ku$_6$] kun-zi	1 pond-grown fish

ending broken

Introduction

The fragmentary text records various food allotments including fish, onion and dates to different individuals. For the discussion of the food from Ur III texts, see H. Brunke, *Essen in Sumer: Metrologie, Herstellung und Terminologie nach Zeugnis der Ur III-zeitlichen Wirtschaftsurkunden* (München: Herbert Utz Verlag, 2011).

Commentary

obv. 2') For the term sag-kur$_2$ or sag-pap, see R. K. Englund, *Organisation und Verwaltung der Ur III-Fischerei* (Berlin: Dietrich Reimer Verlag, 1990), pp. 212–13.

rev. 2–3) For the terms both ku$_6$ ^{gi}hal and gu$_2$ sum sikil, see *BJRL* 64, 116 86; *SAT* 3, 1763; *Aleppo* 469; *Syracuse* 325.

No. 6 – Receipt of dead animals

Shelfmark: JRL 1032
Provenience: Puzrish-Dagan
Date: (AS 3) v 2
Catalogue: Iraq 62, 023 JRL 1032 catalogue

Text

obv.

    1) [. . .]   *(animal)*
    2) 1 maš$_2$-gal   *1 goat*
    3) ba-ug$_7$ *dead*
    4) u$_4$ 2-kam   *on the 2nd day,*

rev.

    1) ki Lu$_2$-[dingir-ra-t]a   *from Lu-dingira*
    2) ^{d}Š[ul-gi]-iri-/m[u]   *Shulgi-irimu*
    3) šu ba-t[i]   *received.*
    4) iti ezem ^{d}Nin-a-[zu]   *Month: 'Festival of Ninazu.'*
    5) mu [. . .]   *Year: [. . .]*

Introduction

This text deals with the receipt of dead animals from Lu-dingira (son of Inim-Shara), an official in the nakabtum branch of the Puzrish-Dagan organisation, dating between Shulgi 46 and Amar-Suen 3. It is noted that this official of the nakabtum branch was different from a homonymous person, Lu-dingira son of Arad-hulla who was also an official in the Puzrish-Dagan organisation exclusively dealing with the wild or rare animals, such as bears (az), bezoars (dara$_4$), cervids (lulim, šeg$_9$-bar) and gazelles (maš-da$_3$). For the administration of Lu-dingira son of Inim-Shara from Puzrish-Dagan archives, see M. Sigrist, *Drehem* (Bethesda: CDL Press, 1992), pp. 325–7; C. Tsouparopoulou, 'A Reconstruction of the Puzriš-Dagan Central Livestock Agency', *Cuneiform Digital Library Journal*, 2 (2013), 1–15; C. Liu, *Organization, Administrative Practices and Written Documentation in Mesopotamia during the Ur III Period (c.2112–2004 BC): A Case Study of Puzriš-Dagan in the Reign of Amar-Suen* (Münster: Ugarit-Verlag, 2017), pp. 271–80.

Commentary

rev. 5) Based both on the fact that Shulgi-irimu received the dead animals from Puzrish-Dagan archives dating between Amar-Suen 3 and Ibbi-Suen 2, and on the fact that the texts from Puzrish-Dagan issued by Lu-dingira son of Inim-Shara date between Shulgi 46 and Amar-Suen 3, it is speculated that dead animals were received by Shulgi-irimu from Lu-dingira son of Inim-Shara only dating to Amar-Suen 3. In other words, there is little doubt that this text dates to Amar-Suen 3. For the officials dealing with dead animals from Puzrish-Dagan archives, see C. Tsouparopoulou, 'Killing and Skinning Animals in the Ur III Period: The Puzriš-Dagan (Drehem) Office Managing of Dead Animals and Slaughter By-products', *Altorientalische Forschungen*, 40 (2013), 150–82.

No. 7 – Dealing with flour

Shelfmark: JRL 1033
Provenience: Umma?
Date: – iv 10
Catalogue: Iraq 62, 023 JRL 1033 catalogue

Text

obv.

beginning broken
1') [...] zi$_3$ [...] flour
2') [ki ... t]a?   from? [...]
3') [...] [x]

rev.

1) [...] zi$_3$ [...] flour
2) [u$_4$] 10-kam   on the 10th day.
space line
3) [iti?] nesag   Month: 'First-fruit offfering'.
4) [mu? ...] KI [...]   Year: [...]

Introduction

This fragmental tablet is difficult to reconstruct. It probably records a transfer of flour from one individual to another one.

Commentary

obv. 1') and rev. 1) The only sign attested in this line is also possibly either U$_8$ or SIG$_2$, or even E.

rev. 3) The only sign attested in this line is most probably to be read as NESAG, a part of the month name 'iti nesag', based on which the provenience of this text is Umma.

No. 8 – Withdrawl of onion

Shelfmark: JRL 1035
Provenience: Umma
Date: SS 1 iii
Catalogue: Iraq 62, 023 JRL 1035 catalogue

Text

obv.

    1) 1(aš) gu$_2$ šum$_2$ sikil?   *1 talent pure onion*
    2) siskur$_2$? a-ša$_3$?   *for rite of the fields?*
    3) zi-ga   *withdrawal.*
    4) x x x x   *…*

rev.

    1) 1 x x x   *1 …*
    2) e$_2$ šu ba-ti?   *received?*
    3) Ur-am$_3$-ma   *Ur-amma.*
    4) iti še-kar-[ra]-/gal$_2$-la mu   *Month: 'Barley at the quay'.*
    ^{d}Šu-^{d}EN./ZU lugal   *Year: 'Shu-Suen was the king'.*

Introduction

The text records that onions were withdrawn by someone and (unclear thing, possibly also onions were) received by Ur-amma.

Commentary

obv. 4 and rev. 1) Based on the photograph available from CDLI, two lines are illegible.

rev. 3) For the individual Ur-amma, who 'enjoyed a long career in Umma' and 'was an cultivator of the governor' (of Umma), see M. Widell, 'Ur III Economy and Bureaucracy: The Neo-Sumerian Cuneiform Tablets in the Hood Museum of Art, Dartmouth College (I)', *Orient*, 55 (2020), 8; M. Stepien, 'The Economic Status of Governors in Ur III Times: An Example of the Governor of Umma', *Journal of Cuneiform Studies*, 64 (2012), 20.

No. 9 – About the fields

Shelfmark: JRL 1088d
Provenience: Irisagrig
Date: ---

Text

obv.

    beginning broken
    1') [a]-ša$_3$ gid$_2$-[da]   *long field*
    2') [gi]r$_3$-si$_3$-ga gu$_4$-a[pin …]   *attendants of plow oxen […]*

rev.

    all broken

Introduction

This fragmental tablet which probably belongs to the pisan-dub-ba text, namely the previous line of obv. 1') is reconstructed as pisan-dub-ba, cf. *CUSAS* 40, 0409; *Nisaba* 15, 0893; both of which are from Irisagrig. For the pisan-dub-ba texts in Ur III period, see R. C. Nelson, 'Pisan-dub-ba Texts from the Sumerian Ur III Dynasty' (PhD dissertation, University of Minnesota, 1976); W. Sallaberger and A. Westenholz, *Mesopotamien: Akkade-Zeit und Ur III-Zeit* (Freiburg: Universitätsverlag, 1999), pp. 214–16. For the Ur III texts from Irisagrig, see D. I. Owen, *Cuneiform Texts Primarily from Iri-Saĝrig/Āl-Šarrākī and the History of the Ur III Period* (Bethesda: CDL Press, 2013).

Commentary

obv. 2') For the term gir$_3$-si$_3$-ga (Akk. *gerseqqûm*) 'palace, temple attendant', see R. K. Englund, 'The Year: "Nissen returns joyous from a distant island"', *Cuneiform Digital Library Journal*, 1 (2003), 4; G. Visicato, *The Bureaucracy of Šuruppak: Administrative Centres, Central Offices, Intermediate Structures and Hierarchies in the Economic Documentation of Fara* (Münster: Ugarit-Verlag, 1995), p. 108; K. Maekawa, 'The Agricultural Texts of Ur III Lagash of the British Museum (V)', *Acta Sumerologica*, 9 (1987), 96–7.

No. 10 – Unclear

Shelfmark: JRL 1088e
Provenience: uncertain
Date: ---

Text

obv.

    all destroyed

rev.

    all destroyed

seal

    1) I$_3$-li$_2$-[tab-ni]   *Ili-tabni*
    2) [dub]-sar   *scribe*
    3) [dumu] I-di$_3$-[DINGIR]   *son of Iddin-ilum*

Introduction

This tablet is wholly unreadable.

Commentary

For the reconstruction of this seal, see D. Collon, *Catalogue of the Western Asiatic Seals in the British Museum: Cylinder Seals II, Akkadian ~ Post Akkadian ~ Ur III Periods* (London: British Museum Publications, 1982), p. 149 (no. 384): I$_3$-li$_2$-tab-ni/dumu I-ti-DINGIR.

No. 11 - Unclear

Shelfmark: JRL 1088f
Provenience: Umma?
Date: ---

Text

obv.

    1) [...]
    2) [...]
    3) [... ^{d}S]uen?   [...]-*Suen*
    4) [... ^{d}N]in-ur$_4$-ra   [...]-*Ninurra*
    5) [... K]I
    ending broken

rev.

    beginning broken
    1') [...] munu$_4$?
    ending broken

Introduction

This fragmental tablet has been heavily damaged and is unreadable.

Commentary

obv. 4) The occurrence of the divine name Ninurra or personal name with Ninurra as a part was mostly attested in Umma texts.

Notes

The work presented here is part of a project supported by the Key Project on Philosophy and Social Sciences of Ministry of Education of China (Grant no. 23JZD040). The authors would like to thank Dr Jeremy Penner, curator of African and Near Eastern Manuscripts at the John Rylands Research Institute and Library, University of Manchester, for permission to publish these texts here and for providing us with great support.

1. For the introduction of the Third Dynasty of Ur, see W. Sallaberger and A. Westenholz, *Mesopotamien: Akkade-Zeit und Ur III-Zeit* (Freiburg: Universitätsverlag, 1999), pp. 121–392; P. Steinkeller, 'The Sargonic and Ur III Empires', in P. F. Bang, C. A. Bayly and W. Scheidel (eds), *The Oxford World History of Empire, Volume 2: The History of Empires* (Oxford: Oxford University Press, 2021), pp. 43–72. The dating in this article follows the middle chronology, for which see J. Reade, 'Assyrian King-Lists, the Royal Tombs of Ur, and Indus Origins', *Journal of Near Eastern Studies*, 60 (2001), 1–29. For the Sumerian King List, see T. Jacobsen, *The Sumerian King List* (Chicago: University of Chicago Press, 1939).
2. M. Molina, 'The Corpus of Neo-Sumerian Tablets: An Overview', in S. J. Garfinkle and J. C. Johnson (eds), The Growth of an Early State in Mesopotamia: Studies in Ur III Administration. Proceedings of the First and Second Ur III Workshops at the 49th and 51st Rencontre Assyriologique Internationale, London, 10 July 2003 and Chicago, 19 July 2005 (Madrid: Consejo Superior de Investigaciones Cientificas, 2008), pp. 19–54; M. Molina, 'Archives and Bookkeeping in Southern Mesopotamia During the Ur III Period', *Revue d'Histoire des Comptabiliteìs*, 8 (2016), 2–19; and statistics by databases both CDLI (https://cdli.mpiwg-berlin.mpg.de/ [accessed 20 January 2024]) and BDTNS (http://bdtns.filol.csic.es/ [accessed 20 January 2024]).
3. https://www.library.manchester.ac.uk/rylands/special-collections/search/published-catalogues/cuneiform/ [accessed 20 January 2024].
4. C. Bedale, *Sumerian Tablets from Umma in the John Rylands Library – Manchester* (Manchester: Manchester University Press, 1915).
5. S. A. B. Mercer, 'Some Babylonian Contracts', *Journal of the Society of Oriental Research*, 12 (1928), 35–41; S. A. B. Mercer, 'Some Babylonian Contracts', *Journal of the Society of Oriental Research*, 13 (1929), 175–80.
6. T. Fish, *Catalogue of Sumerian Tablets in the John Rylands Library* (Manchester: Manchester University Press, 1932).
7. T. Fish, 'Some Sumerian Tablets in the John Rylands Library', *Bulletin of the John Rylands University Library*, 8 (1924), 406–11; T. Fish, 'A Sumerian Wage-List of the Ur Dynasty', *Bulletin of the John Rylands University Library*, 9 (1925), 241–7; T. Fish, 'The Cult of King Dungi During the Third Dynasty of Ur', *Bulletin of the John Rylands University Library*, 11 (1927), 322–8; T. Fish, 'The Contemporary Cult of Kings of the Third Dynasty of Ur', *Bulletin of the John Rylands University Library*, 12 (1928), 75–82; T. Fish, 'A Note on the Min Months in the Drehem Calendar', *Bulletin of the John Rylands University Library*, 13 (1929), 128–30; E. Sollberger, *The Business and Administrative Correspondence under the Kings of*

Ur (Locust Valley: J. J. Augustin, 1966); T. Gomi, *Wirtschaftstexte der Ur III-Zeit aus dem British Museum* (Rome: Multigrafica editrice, 1982); C. Wilcke, 'Flurschäden, verursacht durch Hochwasser, Unwetter, Militär, Tiere und schuldhaftes Verhalten zur Zeit der 3. Dynastie von Ur', in H. Klengel and J. Renger (eds), *Landwirtschaft im alten Orient. Ausgewählte Vorträge der XLI. Rencontre Assyriologique Internationale (Berlin, 4.-8.7.1994)* (Berlin: D. Reimer, 1999), pp. 301-39.

8 T. Donald, 'A Sumerian Plan in the John Rylands Library', *Journal of Semitic Studies*, 7 (1962), 184.

9 T. Gomi, 'Ur III Texts in the John Rylands University Library of Manchester', *Bulletin of the John Rylands University Library*, 64 (1981-82), 87-116.

10 F. al-Rawi, 'Cuneiform Inscriptions in the Collections of the John Rylands Library, University of Manchester', *Iraq*, 62 (2000), 21-63.

University of Manchester Library 23025: A Single-Leaf Print of the Crucifixion from a Late Medieval Etched Metal Plate, or a Nineteenth-Century Forgery?

EDWARD POTTEN, UNIVERSITY OF MANCHESTER

Abstract

Among the small, but highly significant, collection of single-leaf prints amassed by George John, 2nd Earl Spencer (1758–1834), one print has consistently proved controversial. An impression from an etched metal plate, this scene of the Crucifixion bears the 'impossible' date of 1430. The date is not the only issue with the impression; stylistically and materially it is unlike any other produced in the fifteenth century. This article examines the impression afresh, recording a variety of oddities and anomalies. It introduces a new piece of physical evidence – the watermark from the paper on which the impression now at the John Rylands Library was printed – before concluding with some observations on the validity and purpose of this extraordinary print.

Keywords: fifteenth century; metal cuts; woodcuts; etching; single-sheet prints; Hans Albrecht, Freiherr von Derschau; George John, 2nd Earl Spencer

In 1818, during his bibliographical, antiquarian and picturesque tour of Europe with the artist George Robert Lewis (1782–1871), Thomas Frognall Dibdin (1776–1847) visited Hans Albrecht, Freiherr von Derschau (1754–1824) in Nuremberg. While there, he expressed to his host 'a desire to purchase any little curiosity or antiquity, in the shape of a *book* or *print*, for which the Baron had no immediate use'.[1] He was richly rewarded, acquiring 'in the book way', vellum copies of the *Compendium morale* and the *Breviarium Cracoviense*, a copy of the 1496 Grüninger Terence, Erasmus's Greek Testament, an unidentified printed Book of Hours, and copies of a variety of useful European histories, all of which went straight into the library of his patron, George John, 2nd Earl Spencer (1758–1834).[2] 'In the *print* way', Dibdin secured 'a few *Martin Schoens*, *Albert Durers*, and *Israel Van Mechlins*; and … a beautiful little illumination, cut out of an old choral book, or psalter, said, by the vendor, to be the production of *Weimplan*, an artist, at Ulm, of the latter end of the fifteenth century', alongside two extremely interesting printed impressions.[3] The first, a 'dotted print' of St Catherine, considered by Wilhelm Ludwig Schreiber to be one of the earliest prints of this kind to survive, Dibdin sold to Jean Duchesne (1779–1855), Director of the Cabinet des estampes of the Bibliothèque nationale,

Paris.[4] The second was a genuine curiosity, about which Dibdin expounded at length:

> But the Baron laid the greatest stress upon a copper plate impression of a crucifixion, of the date of 1430: which undoubtedly had a very staggering aspect [. . .] I will describe this singular specimen of old art as briefly and perspicuously as I am able. It consists of an impression, in pale black ink – resembling very much that of aquatint, of a subject cut upon copper, or brass, which is about seventeen inches in height (the top being a little cut away) and about ten inches six-eighths in width. The upper part of the impression is in the shape of an obtusely pointed, or perhaps rather semi-circular, gothic window – and is filled by involutions of forms or patterns, with great freedom of play and grace of composition: resembling the stained glass in the upper parts of the more elaborated gothic windows of the beginning of the fifteenth century. Round the outer border of the subject, there are seven white circular holes, as if the metal from which the impression was taken, had been *nailed up* against a wall – and these blank spots were the result of the aperture caused by the space formerly occupied by the nails. Below, is the subject of the crucifixion. The cross is ten inches high: the figure of Christ, without the glory, six inches: St. John is to the left, and the mother of Christ to the right of the cross; and each of these figures is about four inches high. The drawing and execution of these three figures, are barbarously puerile. To the left of St. John is a singular appearance of the *upper* part of *another* plate, running at right angles with the principal, and composed also in the form of the upper portion of a gothic window. To the right of the virgin, and of the plate, is the "staggering" date above mentioned. It is thus: M.C.C.C.C.XXX. This date is fixed upon the stem of a tree, of which both the stem and the branches above appear to have been *scraped*, in the copper, almost *white* – for the sake of introducing the inscription, or *date*. The date, moreover, has a very suspicious look, in regard to the execution of the letters of which it is composed. As to the *paper*, upon which the impression is taken, it has, doubtless, much of the look of old paper; but not of that particular kind, either in regard to *tone* or *quality*, which we see in the prints of Mechlin, Schoen, or Albert Durer. But what gives a more "staggering aspect" to the whole affair is, that the worthy Derschau had *another* copy of this *same* impression, which he sold to Mr. John Payne, and which is now in the highly curious collection of Mr. Douce. This was fortunate to say the least. The copy purchased by myself is now in the collection of Earl Spencer.[5]

Despite the 'barbarously puerile' nature of the impression, Dibdin found himself 'well satisfied with the result of the "temptation" practised upon me at Baron Derschau's', leaving his mansion 'with my purse lightened of about 340 florins'.[6] Spencer was clearly also sufficiently interested to acquire an impression, as was Francis Douce, who acquired the second Derschau impression, identical to the Spencer copy but trimmed to the upper border, now at the Ashmolean Museum.[7]

At least two further impressions are recorded, although their current locations are unknown. Derschau's first collection of woodblocks and impressions was sold en bloc to the King of Prussia in 1817, and forms one of the foundation collections of the Berlin Kupferstichkabinett. His second collection was sold by the Nuremberg auctioneer J. L. Schmidmer after Derschau's death in 1825, and two additional impressions from the 1430 plate merit description in that catalogue.[8] The first is listed under Class I of the German School, among the dated prints as lot 19:

> 1 Bl. Christus am Kreutz, an dessen Stamm zur Rechten die hl. Jungfrau, zur Linken St. Johannes stehen; der Vor- und Hintergrund ist mit Goldschmied-Zierathen bedecket. Zur Rechten stehet auf einem abgebrochenen Stamm, und untereinander gestellet, die Jahrzahl M·C·C·C·.XXX. Ein Abdruck von einer Metall-Platte ... Uralte Arbeit von grober Ausführung eines ungeschickten Goldschmiedes; indessen der älteste bis jetzt bekannte Abdruck von einer Metallplatte mit einer bestimmten Jahrzahl.[9] ['One leaf. Christ crucified, with the Virgin Mary standing to the right of the cross, and St. John to the left; the foreground and background are covered by decorative goldsmith's work. At the right-hand side, on a broken trunk, and positioned below it, the year MCCC.XXX. An impression from a metalcut. An ancient piece undertaken crudely by an unskilled goldsmith; nonetheless the oldest impression hitherto known from a dated metalcut'].

A second impression was offered as lot 2537, listed with another engraving of the Virgin and Child, erroneously dated 1467.[10] No trace of the later history of these two impressions has been forthcoming, nor is there any trace of the plate from which the impressions were taken. It was not among the blocks in Derschau's first collection, nor did it appear in the posthumous auction of his second collection.

The impressions are certainly unusual. The Rylands example is taken on paper, from an etched metal plate depicting the Crucifixion (Figure 1). Christ on the Cross, centre, faces the viewer; on a tablet above his head the inscription INRI [reversed], his loincloth blowing to the left. At the foot of the Cross is Adam's skull and bones. To the right, the Virgin stands with clasped hands facing left, next to a tree which is lettered with the date: M.CCCC.XXX. [reversed]. To the left, St John stands, facing right, with one hand at his waist holding a tablet, on the lower part of which are the initials GH, the other raised to his chin. The top is decorated with a vegetal pattern inside the geometric shapes formed by a network of twisting scrolls, while the dotted base is decorated with large floral tendrils. The top of the plate is rounded, with nine holes around the outer border, indicating that the plate was nailed at some point. As noted by Dibdin, the bottom leftmost portion of the plate was designed in such a way as to incorporate a semi-circular blank space. Around the whole design runs a narrow border, in which there is a spiral band with buds between the coils. This border design runs around the blank space, indicating that it was part of the original design, and one of the nail holes is within the portion of the border which surrounds the blank space, next to the shoulder of St John. Apparently, at a later date, this void was filled with a fragment cut from a similar etched plate with matching vegetal design, perhaps a different plate from the same series.

From Dibdin onwards, most writers have been highly sceptical about the impressions. Describing a photographic reproduction of the Ashmolean impression held by the British Museum in 1879, William Hughes Willshire summed up the prevailing view:

Figure 1 University of Manchester Library 23025 (Schr. 2312). Image © The University of Manchester. All rights reserved.

We are of opinion that the original metal, from an impression from which the photographic copy before us has been taken, was a forgery of comparatively modern times. The peculiar mixture of technics and of the ornamentation of different periods and styles, the bad and almost childish drawing of the two figures by the Cross, the character and work of the tree bearing the date, the date itself and the presence of a portion of a second plate intruding on the other metal, are sufficient in themselves to excite strong suspicion as to the genuine antique character of the engraving. In addition to these circumstances we cannot help being influenced also by the [...] account given by Dr. Dibdin [...] Were it not for the intrinsic characters of the style and work, &c. before mentioned, it might be allowed perhaps that the original metal plate was truly a genuine one of the period of which it asserts itself to be, and was in the possession of

Baron Derschau, who had caused several impressions to be worked off from it, disposing of them when opportunity offered as veritable antiques. But even this more venial crime is not the only one in our opinion which has been here perpetrated. Whether the Baron was *particeps criminis* in the manufacture of the original plate as well as of the modern impressions cannot be determined, but that he knew the impressions he sold were not old ones can scarcely be doubted.[11]

Willshire's successor at the British Museum, Campbell Dodgson, commented of the British Museum photograph that the plate was 'probably a modern forgery', and that Derschau had probably been in possession of the plate and had the impressions struck off. He also, however, noted an interesting feature:

> The fact that not only is the inscription reversed, but the Virgin appears on the right (in this case, the wrong) side, shows that the plate was intended for decorative purposes and not for producing impressions. The photograph has therefore to be placed with impressions from a number of similar plates, ancient or modern, described by Willsh[ire].[12]

Schreiber was similarly inclined: 'Es handelt sich um eine geätzte Platte, die überdies eine modern Fälschung sein dürfte, denn die Jahreszahl ist unmöglich' ('It is an etched plate and likely to be a forgery, as the year is impossible').[13]

However unconvincing the impressions may be, though, there are some oddities which make little sense if they are a conscious forgery. First, Dibdin is correct in asserting that the figures are 'barbarously puerile'; they are crude and poorly defined and certainly do not look like depictions familiar from other late medieval contexts. Of note here are the 'wavy' smiles of the figures, their large chins, the rounded forms of their noses, the curve of the Virgin's bust, and the fact that their garments are A-line rather than rectangular, without the folds one often sees in German depictions, and hemmed above the ankle. The shoes are not poulaines with dramatically pointed toes, as would be expected in a medieval depiction of figures in noble dress.[14] The figures almost look Victorian, which could be seen as evidence of forgery, but seems an odd approach for a forger to have adopted when there were plenty of fifteenth- and sixteenth-century models to copy. Second, there is the fact of that strange void in the design. The metal plate on which the original etching has been made appears to have been cut to fit a very specific shape, one which incorporates a semi-circular gap. This is an extremely odd feature to introduce into a forgery. Third, the insertion of that additional plate replicating the vegetal design into the void – a rather obtrusive feature – seems even more inexplicable. Fourth, the reversed text and the reversed placement of Mary and St John make no sense if this is a forgery.

Finally, there is the unusual shape, with the oval upper border like a gothic window. The Ashmolean impression has been trimmed close to the rounded top and mounted, but the Rylands impression is a full sheet, demonstrating that the etched plate itself was rounded; the chain lines run from top to bottom. One certainly does find many fifteenth-century prints which adopt a rounded, often architectural, upper border, but in these cases, the outer woodcut border is invariably still rectangular. Fifteenth-century prints with rounded tops may exist, but I have struggled

Figure 2 Augsburg, Universitätsbibliothek, Cod. I.3.8o 5, fo. 194r (Schr. 291c). Public domain.

to find any that adopt this form, a shape more commonly encountered in panels, paintings, manuscript illuminations or triptychs. There are a few candidates, all woodcuts. An impression of the Scourging of Christ printed directly into a manuscript now at Augsburg (Figure 2) features a central column supporting a vaulted ceiling with a rounded top and no outer border at head or foot. However, the presence of outer borders to the left and right suggest that all might not be quite as it seems. This appears to be a woodblock cut down to fit the manuscript's format with the upper and lower borders removed, the arch of the ceiling then provided by the colourist.[15] A French Crucifixion on parchment now at the National Gallery of Art (Figure 3) undoubtedly has a rounded top edge, but this is demonstrably a woodcut produced not to print single-leaf prints, but rather for a letterpress book: the recto contains the printed text from a missal.[16]

Figure 3 Washington, DC, The National Gallery of Art Rosenwald Collection, 1943.3.728 (not in Schr.). Public domain.

A tiny Pietà at Uppsala (Figure 4) has a six-sided 'cottage roof' shaped double outer border, but has been trimmed to its outline rather than this shape being a conscious design.[17] A woodcut of St James Major on Horseback in New York has a rounded top, but it is similarly tiny – 70 mm × 61 mm – and likely cut from a sheet of similarly sized woodcut saints.[18] An impression of the Lamentation in Berlin (Figure 5) has a similarly rounded top, but it is now impossible to tell whether this was the shape of the original block, or whether the print was trimmed by the colourist.[19] A Virgin with Child in Munich (Figure 6), impressed on the back of an unused printed indulgence, has a rounded top, but this was originally a larger woodcut, cut to this shape to fit a specific space.[20] There are no doubt other examples, but these few illustrate the

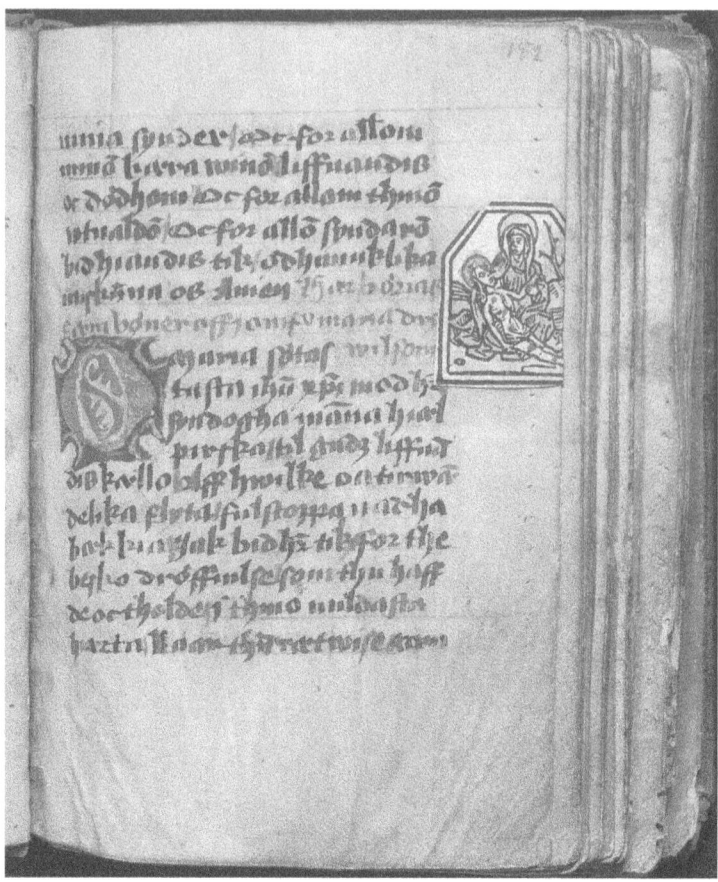

Figure 4 Uppsala, Universitetsbibliotek, UUB C 12, fo. 152r. By permission of Uppsala Universitetsbibliotek. All rights reserved.

trend: this shape was unusual in fifteenth-century block and metal cutting for single-leaf prints, and as often as not, a surviving impression with a rounded top reflects trimming rather than the shape of the original printing medium. The rounded top of the Crucifixion therefore seems an odd affectation for a forger to adopt.

For all these reasons, the plate from which the Rylands impression was taken seems unlikely to be a forgery created as such. The original plate feels made to fit a niche, or to mirror an architectural form. Furthermore, some features of the impression also lend themselves to alternative interpretations, as hinted at by Dodgson. The nail holes here are particularly large and obtrusive. One does find nail holes in metal printing plates of the fifteenth century, where nails were used to attach the plates to a wooden block as part of the printing process, but these are usually small and relatively discrete, and positioned outside the printed design.[21]

Figure 5 Berlin, Staatliche Museen zu Berlin, Kupferstichkabinett, Inv. 69–1 Kupferstichkabinett. Staatliche Museen zu Berlin. Photo: Dietmar Katz. All rights reserved.

The holes in the Crucifixion impression suggest a more robust mounting. The reversed lettering and the placement of the Virgin and St John strongly suggest that this was an impression taken from a decorative plate rather than a surface intended for printing. A number of these anomalous impressions are recorded by Willshire, who describes four such examples at the British Museum where 'it is clear that the original plates were simply ornamental or pictorial ones, and were not intended to be printed from'.[22] The first of these, an Angelic Salutation dated by Willshire to the second half of the fifteenth century, is a modern impression taken from an engraved plate on which everything is similarly reversed. Antonio Maria Zanetti noted the presence of a silver hook and a staple to which a lamp could be attached, indicating the original purpose of the plate.[23] The other three impressions are portraits of Charles V, a duke of Savoy, and Luther – all sixteenth century – all taken from engraved ornamental plates and all apparently the work of one Hans Kellertaler or Kellardarler, a goldsmith and engraver working in Dresden.[24]

Figure 6 Munich, Staatliche Graphische Sammlung, Inv.-Nr. 118216D recto. All rights reserved.

Other examples are known, and there is a long historical debate about whether some of the earliest impressions from metal were in fact taken from decorative plates rather than from plates specifically designed for printing. Two metal cut plates now at the Musée du Louvre (Figure 7) were cited by Schreiber as genuine plates by the Monogrammist 'd'.[25] This anonymous artist is named after the signature 'd', which can be found on two impressions in which the initial and the text incorporated into the design are reversed.[26] Indeed, several of the impressions attributed to the Monogrammist 'd' have reversed text, leading Henri Bouchot to posit that all of these reversed plates were originally intended as decorative plates with paper impressions a sideline.[27] Carl Wehmer later disputed whether the two Louvre plates were genuine in any way ('echt ist an diesem Metallschnitt nur das Kupfer'; 'only the copper is genuine in this metal cut'), based on the erroneous date of 1423 on Schreiber 2746a and errors in the orthography of the texts and in the treatment of the compositions on both plates, but his conclusions are ripe for reanalysis.[28] The text on Schreiber 2746a is reversed, and the presence of a central nail hole in both might

Figure 7 Paris, Musée du Louvre, Département des Objets d'art, OA 2081. By permission of Musée du Louvre, Département des Objets d'art. All rights reserved.

suggest a decorative rather than a printing plate. Elsewhere, a gilded metal plate depicting the Adoration of the Magi in the Staatliche Museen zu Berlin, Kupferstichkabinett, was probably originally part of a metal reliquary altar from the first half of the fifteenth century, but was later repurposed as a printing surface. Two impressions on paper from this plate were noted in 1942 by Otto Fischer.[29] The Herzog August Bibliothek possesses a series of sixteen impressions, the copper plates of which were from the so-called Barbarossa Chandelier in the cupola of the Palatinate Chapel of Aachen Cathedral, made around 1170.[30] The original plates were detached from the chandelier to be printed in 1864. The imprints of nail holes are visible on the edges of the panels. Thus, printing from decorative plates is recognised as a late medieval and later phenomenon.

Figure 8 London, British Museum 1875,0710.185. © The Trustees of the British Museum. All rights reserved.

Dodgson noted stylistic features that indicated to him some parallels between the Crucifixion and another impression from an etched plate in the British Museum, of Adam and Eve, cited by Willshire (Figure 8). Willshire described it thus:

> First half of the sixteenth century. Germany. This print is apparently an impression from an etched iron plate, the work of Hans Burgmair [sic] the younger. The technic has been so managed that some of the forms appear to come white off a black background, and others black from a white one.[31]

Dodgson concluded that the Crucifixion and the Adam and Eve 'may well have been etched by the same hand', the latter having 'the same dotted background ... The two plates have the same ornamental border with curved lines'.[32] The figures of Adam and Eve are better defined, but there are similarities with the Crucifixion. The linkage of the two, however, casts little light on the validity of either. Although Willshire was happy to attribute the print to the sixteenth century and to Burgkmair, it has since been questioned. The current description in the British Museum catalogue states that 'The print has [...] the appearance of a forgery and is most likely a XIXc impression.'[33] Either way, the impression attributed to Burgkmair appears to have been taken from a printing rather than a decorative plate.

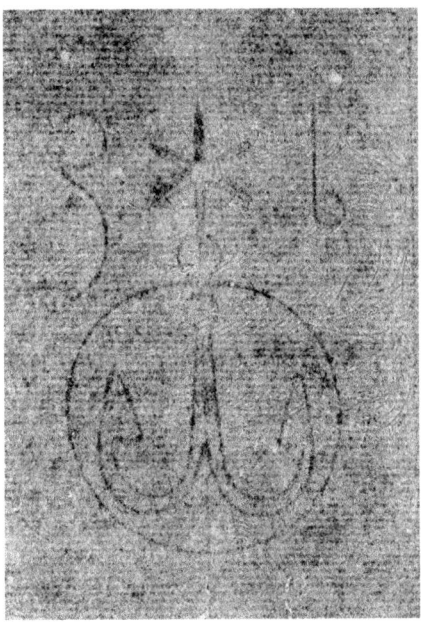

Figure 9 Watermark from University of Manchester Library 23025. © The University of Manchester. All rights reserved.

A fresh examination of the paper on which the known impressions are taken offers an intriguing contribution to the debate. There is no watermark in the Ashmolean impression, but there is a clear watermark in the Rylands impression (Figure 9): an anchor in a circle, surmounted by a star, with an additional motif, a stylised SB, sewn across three chain lines measuring 70 mm (w) × 69 mm (h), with a diameter of 45 mm.[34] This is a very characteristic watermark, and parallels can be found in Gerhard Piccard's printed catalogue of watermarks and in the online Wasserzeichen-Informationssystem.[35] The Crucifixion watermark falls within a bounded group of six examples identified by Piccard.[36] All examples of this cluster, on papers which Piccard believed originated in Northern Italy or Venice, can be dated to 1512–15. Applying the rule established by Piccard that, under normal circumstances, paper produced after *c.*1350 was used within two or at most three years of production, this would suggest that the that the Rylands impression was taken between *c.*1509 and 1518.[37] Thus, despite Dibdin's bold assertion that the paper is 'not of that particular kind, either in regard to *tone* or *quality*, which we see in the prints of Mechlin, Schoen, or Albert Durer', it dates to precisely that period, and incontrovertibly so.

What are we to make of this new evidence? One is left with four possible hypotheses:

1. Both printing surface and impressions are forgeries of the early nineteenth century, printed on paper of the early sixteenth century.
2. The printing surface is a genuine late medieval object bearing, for whatever reason, the date of 1430, and printed in the early sixteenth century.
3. The printing surface is a genuine late medieval object adapted in the early nineteenth century to add the date of 1430 and printed in the early nineteenth century on paper of the early sixteenth century.
4. The printing surface is a genuine decorative plate of indeterminate age, adapted in the early nineteenth century to add the date of 1430 and printed in the early nineteenth century on paper of the early sixteenth century.

The first hypothesis follows Willshire's lead, concluding that, despite the paper evidence, the mash-up of techniques and of ornamentation of different periods and styles, the inept rendering of the two figures by the Cross, and the date, this is most likely an early nineteenth-century forged etched plate. However, this now seems improbable. There are too many oddities relating to the plate to make a conscious forgery likely; if one were creating a forgery from scratch, this is not what one would create. The many anomalies associated with the impression listed by Willshire count against it being an outright forgery. The gothic window shape, the presence of that odd void, the addition of a smaller plate at the bottom left, the reversed text and figures, the unusually large nail holes and the fact of it being an etched plate – these things are so unlikely to be brought together in a forgery that they support the idea that this might be, against all the odds, a genuine impression from a decorative plate.

The second hypothesis relies on the paper evidence. In any other case, one would feel content using the date of the paper as a *terminus post quem* for the creation of the printing surface. To support this, however, one must tackle the single most glaring anomaly – the 1430 date – and the stylistic oddities. Taking the date at face value for a moment, one could argue that dated early fifteenth-century prints are so rare, there is effectively no parallel against which to compare. However, the Crucifixion looks so glaringly unlike any of the very small number of surviving prints that we can confidently date to the 1430s that it must be concluded that the date simply cannot be the date of creation. There are around six dozen woodcut impressions that can securely be dated to before 1440, none of which bear any stylistic similarity to the Rylands impression.[38] Engraved printing plates were being produced by the Master of the Playing Cards in the Upper Rhine area *c.*1435, but again, these bear no stylistic similarity.[39] Prints made in the dotted manner, also known as the *manière criblé*, or *Schrotschnitt*, rather than engraved or etched, date to the 1450s, and again bear no relation to the Rylands impression. Printing from etched plates begins much later in the fifteenth century.

Ad Stijnman cites Daniel Hopfer, an Augsburg armourer, as a pioneer in etching flat iron plates in order to print from them like copper engravings in the mid-1490s.[40] He notes that the Crucifixion plate is similar stylistically to some of the Hopfer etched iron plates, specifically in the use of white dots to fill up the areas around figures and ornamentation, but that it does not show any signs of roughly pitted rust, as is common for iron plates that are printed in intaglio.[41] This, coupled with the shallow etching, suggests that the Crucifixion impression was taken from an etched copper plate. The earliest etchings on copper plates were created by Marcantonio Raimondi and Lucas van Leyden between 1515 and 1520.[42] Thus, even if one could ignore the stylistic impossibilities, the mere fact that the Rylands impression is taken from an etched metal plate reinforces the impossibility of the date indicating the year of design or production.

Are there alternative hypotheses that might explain the presence of an early date on a later plate, and yet still fit chronologically with the paper evidence? It is perhaps pertinent that in the very few cases where prints bear early dates, those dates have been proven to relate to something other than the date of creation. For example, one of Earl Spencer's greatest acquisitions, the Buxheim *Saint Christopher*, a woodcut long claimed as the earliest piece of dated Western printing, was not printed in 1423.[43] The date of 1418 on a *Madonna with Female Saints* has been considered erroneous since Schreiber's description.[44] Arthur Hind succinctly summarises the stylistic links between this woodcut and others dated to 1460–70, before concluding that 'it would be a more reasonable explanation that an early copyist had repeated the date of his original'.[45] Richard Field has convincingly argued that the 1437 on a woodcut of the *Martyrdom of Saint Sebastian* does not represent the date when the block was cut, and the 1446 that appears on a *Saint Nicholas of Tolentino* is more likely to relate to the year of the saint's canonisation rather than the date of the woodcut.[46]

Any date that appears on an early block or plate must be treated with caution, but here the problem is compounded by the fact that the style of the inscription is as implausible as its date. This simply does not look like a Germanic inscription of the fifteenth or early sixteenth century; it looks like a date added in the late eighteenth or early nineteenth century. A technical analysis supports this. Ad Stijnman has suggested that there are two processes at play here: an etched surface producing the decorative design with the date added with a burin.[47] Consequently, a third hypothesis might be that the etched plate is late medieval, with the date added with a burin in the early nineteenth century, then printed on paper of the early sixteenth century. This would explain the addition of the 'impossible' date, but for this to be credible one must explain the paper evidence. An unscrupulous dealer in the early nineteenth century may have sourced paper that was suitably aged on which to take impressions; Dibdin himself commented – albeit incorrectly – on the paper, evidence that connoisseurs were aware in his day that this was a way of distinguishing the genuine from the modern. However, the choice of paper here is notable. The study of watermarks was in its infancy in 1818, so the forger must have been either extremely conscientious or extremely fortuitous in selecting paper for the impression which dates to c.1510 and 1517, precisely the moment when the earliest etchings on copper plates were appearing.

There is, however, also the suspicious fact of Derschau owning not one, but all four of the known impressions to be accounted for. One is mindful of Willshire's critique of Derschau, and his suggestion that he may have been '*particeps criminis* in the manufacture of the original plate as well as of the modern impressions'.[48] The coincidence of all four impressions emanating from Derschau is interesting, and implies that, whatever the date of the original plate, those impressions might originate in Nuremberg, c.1800. Although, this evidence is not necessarily damning – there are other examples of clutches of early impressions surviving together – when considered alongside the burin-added date, it is hard not to put two and two together.[49]

With all this in mind, the most likely hypothesis seems to be that the printing surface is a genuine decorative plate of indeterminate age, adapted in the early nineteenth century to add the date of 1430 and printed in the early nineteenth century on paper of the early sixteenth century. This hypothesis explains the oddity and reversed nature of the plate – it is a repurposed object, rather than an outright forgery – it explains the date added with a burin, and it explains how all four impressions ended up with Derschau in c.1800. If this is indeed a decorative plate, adapted with the addition of the date, then what is it and when was it made? The nail holes show that the metal plate was at some point affixed, perhaps to a pew or to a chest, or attached to a book binding, where it would have been susceptible to damage. Within a devotional context, a plate such as this could have been cut to fit an aumbry or attached to the door of a ciborium cupboard, where the touching, and hence wearing, of the figures may have held a particular resonance.[50] The date of the plate is ultimately a matter of conjecture, but it is hard to reconcile the many stylistic problems evident with a very early date. Most likely, it is the work of an unskilled artist and etcher of a later period, creating an etched decorative plate to fit a very specific shape.

Ultimately, as is so often the case with single-leaf impressions, the evidence is not conclusive enough to be certain of much. It is my belief, however, that these impressions were taken from a genuine repurposed decorative artefact, which had done prior service in some other capacity, and was adapted with the addition of the date to pique antiquarian interest during the bibliomania. Although the date may be forged, the object is not. Instead, it joins a growing list of woodblocks, metal plates, and other artefacts that defy classification as outright forgeries. These objects were repurposed, or sometimes newly created, not only to serve the needs of collectors, but also as tools for an emerging antiquarian community actively creating the new discipline of book history.[51] Understood in this context, they merit much further study.

Notes

The author is grateful to Stephen Mossman, Roger Gaskell, Elizabeth Savage, Richard Linenthal and Ad Stijnman for their comments and observations on the Rylands impression, and to Nathalie Coilly.

1 Thomas Frognall Dibdin, *A bibliographical antiquarian and picturesque tour in France and Germany ... Second edition*, vol. 3 (London: published by Robert Jennings and John Major, 1829), p. 443. The same text appeared in the first edition, vol. 3 (London: Printed for the author, by W. Bulmer and W. Nicol, Shakspeare Press, and sold by Payne and Foss, Longman, Hurst and Co., 1821), supplement, pp. xxxiv–xxxvi.

2 Antonius Rampigollis, *Compendium morale* ([Augsburg: Monastery of SS. Ulrich and Afra, not after 1473]), ISTC ir00022000, University of Manchester Library (henceforth: UML) 18034; *Breviarium Cracoviense* (Nuremberg: Georg Stuchs for Johann Haller, Cracow, 19 May 1498), ISTC ib01158450, UML 19269; Publius Terentius Afer, *Comoediae* (Strasbourg: Johann (Reinhard) Grüninger, 1 November 1496), ISTC it00094000, UML 3271; *Novum instrumentum omne diligenter ab Erasmo Roterodamo recognitum una cum annotationibus* (Basle: J. Froben, 1516), UML 5543; Hieronymus Pez, *Scriptores rerum Austriacarum veteres ac genuine* (Leipzig, Regensburg: s.n., 1721–45), UML 18330; Simon Schard, *Germanicarum rerum quatuor celebriores vetustioresque chronographi* (Frankfurt: Georg Rab, Sigmund Feyerabend and the heirs of Weigand Han, 1566), not traced at UML; Johann Pistorius, *Rerum Germanicarum scriptores aliquot insignes, a Carolo Magno ad Carolum V. usque* (Regensburg: [s.n.], 1726) UML 18331.

3 Dibdin, *Tour*, pp. 443–6. The illumination was sold by Dibdin to William Young Ottley (1771–1836).

4 Presumably: Wilhem Ludwig Schreiber, *Handbuch der Holz- und Metallschnitte des XV. Jahrhunderts* (Stuttgart: A. Hiersemann; Nendeln, Liechtenstein: Kraus Reprint Corp., 1969–76), vol. 5, no. 2569. Paris, Bibliothèque nationale, RESERVE EA-5 (8)-BOITE ECU. The BnF catalogue suggests that this impression was acquired in 1811 from 'M. Silvestre', but this must be the impression sold by Dibdin to Duchesne in 1818.

5 Dibdin, *Tour*, pp. 444–6, note [cross].

6 *Ibid.*, p. 446.

7 Oxford, Ashmolean Museum, WA1863.1940.

8 J. L. Schmidmer, *Verzeichniss der Seltenen Kunst-Sammlungen von Oehlgemälden, geschmelzten Glasmalereyen, Majolika, Kunstwerken in Bronze u.a. Metallen, in Elfenbein, Wallrosszahn, Holz u. a. Massen, Gefäsen von Rubinfluss, mathematischen Instrumenten, geschnittenen Steinen, Handzeichnungen, Wassermalereyen mit Gold aufgehöht, Malereyen, Wappen, Zeichnungen und Handschriften aus Stammbüchern, illuminirten mit Gold aufgehöhten Kupferstichen und Holzschnitten, Kupferstichen und Holzschnitten aus allen Schulen, Manuscripten und Büchern aus den Hauptfächern der Wissenschaften des dahier verstorbenen Königlich-Preusischen Hauptmanns Herrn Hans Albrecht von Derschau* (Nuremberg: bei dem verpflichteten Auctionator Schmidmer, [1825]).

9 Schmidmer, *Derschau*, Zweite Abtheilung. Kupferstiche und Holzschnitte aus allen Schulen, p. 4, no. 19.
10 *Ibid.*, p. 271. The impression does not appear in the reprints struck from Derschau blocks issued in a series of fascicules under the editorship of Rudolf Zacharias Becker (Rudolf Zacharias Becker (ed.), *Holzschnitte alter deutscher Meister: in den Original-Platten gesammelt von Hans Albrecht von Derschau* (Gotha: bey dem Herausgeber, 1808–16), but as a metal cut it would not have been included.
11 William Hughes Willshire, *A descriptive catalogue of early prints in the British Museum*, vol. 1 (London: Longmans & Co., 1879), pp. 77–9.
12 Campbell Dodgson, *Catalogue of the early German and Flemish woodcuts preserved in the Department of Prints and Drawings in the British Museum*, vol. 1 (London: Longmans & Co., 1903), pp. 170, 206.
13 Schreiber, *Handbuch*, vol. 5, no. 2312.
14 I give thanks to one of the anonymous peer reviewers for this observation.
15 Augsburg, Universitätsbibliothek, Cod. I.3.8.5, fol. 194r, https://nbn-resolving.org/urn:nbn:de:bvb:384-uba002015-0#0393, Schreiber, *Handbuch*, vol. 1, no. 291c.
16 Washington, DC, The National Gallery of Art Rosenwald Collection, 1943.3.728, not in Schreiber, *Handbuch*; https://www.nga.gov/collection/art-object-page.3943.html.
17 Uppsala, Universitetsbibliotek, UUB C 12, fol. 152r, Schreiber, *Handbuch*, vol. 2, no.981b.
18 New York, Metropolitan Museum of Art, 16501.1504-1, Schreiber, *Handbuch*, vol. 8, no. *1504a. See: Wilhelm Ludwig Schreiber, *Holzschnitte, Schrotblätter und Teigdruck des XV. Jahrhunderts der Sammlung James C. McGuire in New York* (Strasbourg: J.H. Ed. Heitz, 1928–1930), vol. 1, taf. 27.
19 Berlin, Staatliche Museen zu Berlin, Kupferstichkabinett, 16201.508, Schreiber, *Handbuch*, vol. 1, no. 508: 'Infolge der starken Bemalung lässt sich nicht feststellen, ob bereits der Holzstock oben abgerundet war oder ob der Illuminator die Abrungdung vorgenommen hat' ('Due to the thick painting, it is not possible to determine whether the woodblock was rounded at the top, or whether the illuminator applied the rounding').
20 Munich, Staatliche Graphische Sammlung, Inv.-Nr. 118216D, Schreiber, *Handbuch*, vol. 1, no. 1088. See: Achim Riether, *Einblattholzschnitte des 15. Jahrhunderts Bestand der Staatlichen Graphischen Sammlung München* (Munich: Staatliche Graphischen Sammlungen München, [2019]), no. 104 and illustration on p. 125. There are many similar examples of prints trimmed to shape; see, for example, Oxford, Ashmolean, WA1863.1881, Schreiber, vol. 8, 1076a, which is clearly a rectangular woodcut, trimmed to result in a six-sided shape: https://www.ashmolean.org/collections-online#/item/ash-object-285452.
21 See, for example, Peter Schmidt, *Gedruckte Bilder in handgeschriebenen Büchern: zum Gebrauch von Druckgraphik im 15. Jahrhundert* (Cologne: Böhlau, 2003), p. 274, where the nail holes in the metal plates used to print the Stöger Passion are used as a means of establishing a chronology of printing.
22 Willshire, *Catalogue*, p. 326.

23 *Ibid.*, pp. 326–7; Antonio Maria Zanetti, *Le premier siècle de la calcographie* (Venice: J. Antonelli, 1837), p. 142.
24 Willshire, *Catalogue*, pp. 328–30.
25 Schreiber, *Handbuch*, vol. 5, no. 2746a (Paris, Musée du Louvre, Département des Objets d'art, OA 2081) and vol. 6, no. 2865 (Paris, Musée du Louvre, Département des Objets d'art, OA 6299); with thanks to Christine Chabod, Musée du Louvre.
26 Schreiber, *Handbuch*, vol. 5, nos 2375 and 2407.
27 See, for example, Schreiber, *Handbuch*, vol. 5, nos 2745, 2746 and 2747. Henri Bouchot, 'Über Einige Inkunabeln des Kupferstichs aus dem Gebiete vou Douia', *Zeitschrift für bildende Kunst*, N.F., Bd. 15 (1904), 58–63.
28 See Carl Wehmer, 'Zur Echtheitskritik der Metallschnittplatten Schreiber 2746a und S. 2865', in Kunze Horst (ed.), *Buch und Papier. Buchkundliche und papiergeschichtliche Arbeiten. H. Bockwitz zum 65. Geburtstage dargebracht* (Leipzig: O. Harrassowitz, 1949), pp. 143–57, the quotation from p. 153. Wehmer believed the Louvre plates were outright forgeries but also introduced a new hypothesis to explain the reversed nature of impressions attributed to the Monogrammist 'd'. In his opinion the reversed plates were not decorative, but neither were they intended for printing, instead created as matrices for producing *Teigdrucke*, paste prints. These rare prints were presumably produced by pasting paper with a thick layer of an oily resin, which could include traces of coloured pigment. A thin layer of metal foil was applied, which could be coated with a lacquer, perhaps shellac, and black ink; a metal plate was then impressed onto the paste. Wehmer suggests that the reversed plates were matrices for creating softer metal plates, which were then impressed onto the pasted paper. On *Teigdrucke*, see Rainer Schoch, 'The Virgin and Child in a Glory', in Peter Parshall and Rainer Schoch (eds), *Origins of European Printmaking: Fifteenth-Century Woodcuts and Their Public* (New Haven, CT: Yale University Press, 2005), p. 90. Wehmer's hypotheses on the Louvre plates have been questioned by Séverine Lepape, who concluded 'Ils ne constituent pas d'éléments sérieux permettant de douter de l'authencitié de la plaque': Séverine Lepape, *Les origines de l'estampe en Europe du Nord* (Paris: Louvre éditions, [2013]), p. 112.
29 Berlin, Staatliche Museen zu Berlin, Kupferstichkabinett, inv no. 7098; see *Late Gothic: The Birth of Modernity* (Berlin: Staatliche Museen zu Berlin, Preussischer Kulturbesitz/ Hatje Cantz [2021]), no. 46, pp. 132–3.
30 Wolfenbüttel, Herzog August Bibliothek, Uk 2° 2 Taf. 1–16.
31 Willshire, *Catalogue*, p. 325, E 12. London, British Museum 1875,0710.185.
32 Dodgson, *Catalogue*, p. 170.
33 https://www.britishmuseum.org/collection/object/P_1875-0710-185.
34 The author is grateful to Caroline Palmer, Print Room Manager in the Western Art Print Room at the Ashmolean Museum, for confirming the absence of a watermark.
35 Gerhard Piccard, *Die Wasserzeichenkartei Piccard im Hauptstaatsarchiv Stuttgart Findbuch VI Wasserzeichen Anker* (Stuttgart: Kohlhammer, 1978); https://www.wasserzeichen-online.de/wzis/index.php.
36 Anker, V, 151–6. AT3800-PO-119031 (https://www.wasserzeichen-online.de/?ref=AT3800-PO-119031); AT3800-PO-119033 (https://www.wasserzeichen-online.de/?ref=AT3800-PO-119033); AT3800-PO-119034 (https://www.wasserzeichen-online.de/?

ref=AT3800-PO-119034); AT3800-PO-119172 (https://www.wasserzeichen-online.de/?ref=AT3800-PO-119172); DE6300-PO-119026 (https://www.wasserzeichen-online.de/?ref=DE6300-PO-119026).

37 See Gerhard Piccard, 'Die Wasserzeichenforschung als historische Hilfswissenschaft', in *Archivalische Zeitschrift* 52 (1956), 62–115, and Alois Haidinger, 'Datieren mittelalterlicher Handschriften mittels ihrer Wasserzeichen', *Anzeiger der Österreichischen Akademie der Wissenschaften, phil.-hist. Klasse* 139 (2004), 5–30.

38 Richard Field, 'Early Woodcuts: The Known and the Unknown', in Parshall and Schoch, *Origins*, p. 20.

39 Ad Stijnman, *Engraving and Etching 1400–2000* (London: Archetype Publications; Houten, Netherlands: In association with HES and DE GRAAF Publishers, 2012), p. 31.

40 *Ibid.*, p. 52. See also Nadine M. Orenstein and Ad Stijnman, 'Bitten with Spirit: Etching Materials and Techniques in the Sixteenth Century', in Catherine Jenkins, Nadine M. Orenstein and Freyda Spira (eds), *The Renaissance of Etching* (New York: The Metropolitan Museum of Art, [2019]), pp. 15–25; and Christof Metzger, 'The Iron Age: The Beginnings of Etching about 1500', in Jenkins, Orenstein, and Spira (eds), *The Renaissance of Etching*, pp. 25–7.

41 Ad Stijnman, personal communication, August 2024. See, for example, Daniel Hopfer, Medallion with grape vines, strawberry plants and grotesques, Amsterdam, Rijksmuseum, RP-P-1919-2007: http://hdl.handle.net/10934/RM0001.COLLECT.446821

42 Stijnman, *Engraving*, p. 54.

43 See Edward Potten, 'A Succession of Uncertainties: Dating the Buxheim *Saint Christopher*', in John Goldfinch, Takako Kato and Satoko Tokunaga (eds), *Production and Provenance: Copy-specific Features of Incunabula* (Library of the Written Word, 123/Handpress World, 101) (Leiden, Boston: Brill, 2024), pp. 51–79.

44 Schreiber, *Handbuch*, vol. 2, no. 1160.

45 Arthur Mayger Hind, *An Introduction to a History of the Woodcut*, vol. 1 (London: Constable, 1935), p. 111. Peter Schmidt concludes that there is no evidence of Western woodblock impressions on paper or parchment prior to the 1420s, and states that the *Madonna with Female Saints* 'cannot have been made before 1460': Peter Schmidt, 'The Multiple Image: The Beginnings of Printmaking, between Old Theories and New Approaches', in Parshall and Schoch, *Origins*, p. 39.

46 Schreiber, *Handbuch*, vol. 3, no. 1684, Richard Field, 'The Martyrdom of Saint Sebastian', in Parshall and Schoch, *Origins*, pp. 157–8; Schreiber, vol. 3, no. 1637. Peter Schmidt, 'Manuscript with the "Buxheim" Saint Christopher', Parshall and Schoch, *Origins*, p. 153.

47 Ad Stijnman, personal communication, August 2024.

48 See note 11.

49 Two impressions of a remarkable dotted print of Christ on the Mount of Olives ended up together in a copy of the Gutenberg Bible printed on vellum, now Huntington Library 92588. Peter Schmidt cites several prints owned in multiple copies in manuscripts from Tegernsee. Paulus Steger, a brother at Tegernsee, for example, pasted two copies of a metal cut Calvary into a Breviary; Schmidt lists a further eight examples. See Schmidt, *Gedruckte Bilder*, pp. 168–70. There are also many examples of ephemeral

letterpress printed sheets surviving in batches. See, for example, Sixtus IV's letter *Quoniam civitas et insula Rhodi* (1 July 1480) printed as a broadside by Peter Drach in Speyer (ISTC is00561000; GW M4248010), all known copies of which were found within a copy of Leonardus de Utino, *Sermones de Sanctis* ([Strasbourg: Martin Schott, not after 1481]; ISTC il00163000; GW M17901), now Stuttgart, Württembergische Landesbibliothek, Inc. fol. 16126 (HB).

50 The possibility of this being a metal plate from the door of a ciborium cupboard was mentioned in the 1825 Derschau auction catalogue: 'Ein Abdruck von einer Metall-Platte, so ehemals wahrscheinlich an der Thür eines Ciborien-rankes befestiget gewesen, wie sieben um den Rand der Platte ansichtliche Löcher ausweisen' ['An impression of a metal plate, which was probably formerly attached to the door of a ciborium cabinet, as shown by seven visible holes around the edge of the plate']; Schmidmer, *Derschau*, Zweite Abtheilung. Kupferstiche und Holzschnitte aus allen Schulen, p. 4, no. 19.

51 See, for example, the author's discussion of several 'late medieval' woodblocks commissioned by the English antiquarian John Bagford (1650/51–1716) around 1706–07, Elizabeth Savage's discussion of a pair of 'early sixteenth-century' woodblocks collected by Derschau, in fact designed shortly before *c.*1810, and several new 'old' woodblocks commissioned by the German print historian Joseph Heller (1798–1849) to illustrate his histories of print. Such woodblocks have traditionally been seen as fakes or forgeries, but they are not: they were created as research tools to understand technique, explore the mechanics of printing, and replicate and celebrate the earliest Western European prints. See Edward Potten, 'Dating the Rylands Apocalypse Wood-block: John Bagford and the Earliest Facsimiles of Blockbooks', *Journal of the Printing Historical Society*, 3rd series, 3 (2022), 14–46; Elizabeth Savage, "Early Modern' Woodblocks or Antiquarian Homages? A New Date for the Derschau Colour Woodcut *Landsknechte*', in Elizabeth Savage and Femke Speelberg (eds), *Printing Things: Studying Blocks, Plates, and Other Objects from Western Print Heritage* (Oxford: Oxford University Press, 2025). Heller's collection of authentic and recreated woodblocks and copperplates can be viewed through the Staatsbibliothek Bamberg, http://digital.bib-bvb.de/collections/SBB/#/collection/DTL-5754).

Adaption and Experimentation: The Evolution of Charles Calvert's Acting Edition of *The Tempest*

IAN MARTIN NICKSON,
UNIVERSITY OF MANCHESTER

Abstract

This article focuses on a copy of the hitherto unknown acting edition of Charles Calvert's *The Tempest* in the catalogue of the University of Kent's Pettingell Collection that offers new insights into Calvert's Shakespearean revivals in Manchester. It begins by considering the metropolitan influences from which Calvert derived the approach to his revivals, before discussing his experimental adaptations from British, French and American melodramas, culminating in him writing his own original play, *The Hive of Life*, between his exit from the Theatre Royal in 1860 and his appointment as actor-manager at the Prince's Theatre in 1864. It then turns to Calvert's acting edition of *The Tempest*, explaining how and why he wished to adhere to the 'genuine' text, reversing most of Charles Kean's changes, which he had applied for his revival at London's Princess's Theatre in 1857. Finally, it demonstrates how these amendments contributed to the revival's commercial success, something which had eluded Calvert's illustrious predecessors.

Keywords: Charles Calvert; Shakespeare; The Tempest; melodrama; adaptation

Anyone reading the following comments from a review of the opening night of Calvert's first Shakespearean revival, *The Tempest*, in October 1864 would be forgiven for thinking that his production consisted of nothing more than the slavish importation of ideas and expertise from London. 'Mr. Grieve, of London' had created the scenery; the 'drop scene' or act-drop – the painted cloth which closed the proscenium opening between the acts of a play – had been created by William Roxby Beverley, scenic designer at Covent Garden Drury Lane; 'Mr. Wallerstein, of the St. James's Theatre, had arranged the exquisite musical accompaniment', music which had apparently been plundered from existing works by Arne, Purcell and Arthur Sullivan.[1] Another account seems to indicate that the scenery and properties had been transferred from a London theatre, the production being performed 'with all the scenic effects which were so much admired at the Princess's during Mr. Charles Kean's management'.[2]

This article argues that this was far from being the case, however, by showing how Calvert's Manchester production made a number of key innovations that went well beyond anything that had been attempted by Kean in London. I describe how Calvert's experience as an actor in the provinces and as a theatre manager in London gave him insights into the standards attained by metropolitan theatres and the challenges of performing in provincial locations. I then provide an account of his adaptations of American, French and British melodramas and explain how their financial and critical success informed the approach to his Shakespearean revivals in Manchester.

By comparing Calvert's acting edition of *The Tempest* with that created by Charles Kean for his revival at the Princess's Theatre in London, I demonstrate that Calvert's approach to staging revivals combined the best of Kean and Samuel Phelps with his own contributions, creating spectacular, historically accurate theatre that was not only the artistic and aesthetic equal of anything metropolitan theatres could offer, but was consistently profitable. I examine how Calvert's acting edition of *The Tempest* stands as testimony to his desire that his acting editions should be made educational as well as entertaining by including extensive footnotes and explanations, just as Kean had done. However, Calvert went beyond Kean's practice by creating a version of the text that would support two ambitions: first, the creation of a 'one-nation' Shakespeare that would attract all sections of society to the theatre by preserving the essence of Shakespeare's moral messages and characterisations, and second, the transformation of Shakespeare's plays into a predictably profitable enterprise, something that had eluded even eminent theatre managers such as Kean.

Some explanation of the unique status of Calvert's acting edition of *The Tempest* is required. Acting editions of most of Calvert's revivals were sold to the general public for sixpence at the theatre box office and bookshops. The absence from the archives of an acting edition of *The Tempest*, Calvert's first Shakespearean revival in 1864, might lead one to believe that one had not been published, since the commercial success of his revivals had not yet been established. However, in the online catalogue of the University of Kent's Pettingell Collection is an entry for 'Shakespeare's comedy of *The Tempest*'. The item lacks its front and rear covers, and no other copies have come to light, so the publisher and place of publication remain unknown since; I nevertheless attempt to establish a publication date later in this article.

Previous scholars have overlooked Calvert's text of *The Tempest*, since it is missing from the more well-known, and so more frequently consulted, archives of New York University, the New York Public Library for the Performing Arts, the Shakespeare Birthplace Trust and the Folger Shakespeare Library, who collectively curate copies of all his other acting editions. Locally, the John Rylands Library in Manchester holds the only known bound volume of Calvert's acting editions, but even this lacks *The Tempest*, while the catalogue of Manchester's Central Library lists five acting editions, again without *The Tempest*.

This archival discovery enables me to build on the limited scholarship devoted to Calvert's career, notably Richard Foulkes's *The Calverts: Actors of Some Importance* (1992), the first and, to this day, only detailed analysis of his career. An examination of the manuscript and playbill sources cited by Foulkes shows that he had not had access to Calvert's text for *The Tempest*, and so was unable to explore fully this phase of his career or assess its influence on his later revivals.[3] For the same reason, more recent scholarship such as Virginia Vaughan's *The Tempest: Shakespeare in Performance* (2011) overlooks Calvert's contributions to the play's theatrical history. The rediscovery of Calvert's acting edition of *The Tempest* thus enables me for the first time to discern Calvert's transition from melodrama to sophisticated and innovative Shakespearean revival, and to demonstrate how the text of *The Tempest* reveals his cautious, conservative, derivative approach to his first revival.

Metropolitan Influences

Providing an accurate and comprehensive nineteenth-century performance history of *The Tempest* is impossible, since the published literature concentrates on theatres in London and its suburbs. Provincial theatrical productions have traditionally been overlooked by academic researchers, perhaps influenced by Odell's comments, written in 1920, that, between 1859 and 1879, Shakespeare's plays appeared on the stage in Britain only in 'a series of scattered performances at various theatres, Drury Lane being the most conspicuous'.[4] Although this article cannot hope to repair this gap in our appreciation of provincial Shakespearean performances, it aims to raise awareness of their significance and to encourage further studies into them. It is fortunate, therefore, that the influences that shaped Calvert's early career are exclusively metropolitan, so that the deficiency in the available literature is not to the detriment of this article.

In his 1807 review of John Philip Kemble's production of *The Tempest*, based on Dryden's version of the play, at Covent Garden, the English critic, essayist and poet, Leigh Hunt, charged that Dryden had 'filled the dialogue … with obscene double meanings and innuendoes, which he had contrived to render as disgusting as possible by putting them in the mouths of two innocent virgins'.[5] The critic and essayist William Hazlitt complained that Kemble had 'thought fit and necessary to modernise the original play, and to disfigure its simple and beautiful structure, by loading it with … all the heavy tinsel and affected formality which Dryden had borrowed from the French school'.[6] By the early nineteenth century, versions such as Dryden's were no longer in tune with public taste. Shakespeare was by now revered as the national poet while the theatre had become a national pastime, sometimes with intensely patriotic overtones. Productions of Shakespeare's plays enabled the stage to fulfil its role as a 'self-consciously nationalistic form of social practice … [and] theatre-going was an informal act of mass public patriotism, a chance to luxuriate in the display of English virtue'.[7] In response to these changed cultural trends, attempts were made to restore Shakespeare's characterisations and plots by being faithful to the original texts.

In the vanguard of this movement was William Charles Macready, who in advance of the 1838–39 season announced revivals of several of Shakespeare's plays 'in the genuine text of the poet' with the aim of attaining 'the utmost fidelity of historic illustration'.[8] Indeed, Macready's *The Tempest* ran for fifty-five nights, confirming the popular appeal of his approach. However, Macready's management career was combative and financially unsuccessful. At Covent Garden during 1838, his attempts to produce operas and farces as attractive afterpieces were not successful, with his worst setback being the failure of that year's Christmas pantomime, on which he had expended £1,500. Despite these problems, Macready would have been willing to undertake a third year of management but for a dispute with the proprietors of the theatre, who had objected to his unauthorised subleasing of it to the Anti-Corn Law League. Consequently, the proprietors informed him that they planned to re-let the theatre and expected his resignation.[9]

Charles Kean, an Irish-born actor and theatre manager, adopted Macready's approach for his own Shakespearean revivals at London's Princess's Theatre. All of these met with popular acclaim, and Kean's pursuit of realism and historical accuracy as a means of creating serious theatre secured his personal and professional status and election as a Fellow of the Society of Antiquaries.[10] Even so, they failed to make his theatre a profitable enterprise; his first seven seasons generated a combined profit of £2,627, or just over a one per cent return from a £250,000 outlay. Subsequent seasons made money and lost it. In addition, the Panic of 1857 – a financial crisis which began in the United States in September of that year and prompted a run on banks in London, Liverpool and Glasgow the following month – exacerbated a deficit of £4,000 incurred during the 1857–58 season.[11] On 29 August 1859, in his farewell speech, Kean described the financial challenges with which he had been confronted when managing a theatre too small to be remunerative:

> But to carry out my system of pictorial illustration, the cost has been enormous, far too great for the limited arena in which it was incurred. As a single proof I may state that in this little theatre where £200 is considered a large receipt, and £250 an extraordinary one, I expended in one season alone a sum little short of £50,000.[12]

He made it clear that his retirement had not been prompted by lack of desire or popular support, but by financial pressures: 'the pitcher goes so often to the well, but the pitcher at last may be broken'.[13]

A more substantial influence on Calvert than either Kemble, Macready or Kean was Samuel Phelps, whom he had admired from an early age. In 1844, at the age of 16, Calvert and his 13-year-old friend John Coleman stood at the stage door of the Sadler's Wells theatre, with the aim of meeting Phelps on the night that the theatre opened under his management. Phelps, despite being busy with preparations for *Macbeth*, met the two boys and 'gave himself no tragic or autocratic airs, but was gracious and patient'.[14] His management of the Sadler's Wells theatre in Islington was, like Kean's, distinguished by its devotion to Shakespeare. In eighteen years, Phelps produced thirty-one of his plays, fourteen of them in the 1856–57 season alone. Like Kean, his productions were aesthetically pleasing, but unlike Kean, he did not spend lavishly on them and so, despite his theatre being remote from London's West End, his business model proved profitable. Phelps also perpetuated some of the best practices of William Macready, who had insisted on thorough rehearsals and unified productions. As Michael Booth stated, 'through Phelps, the best in Macready's practice was passed on to the next generation, not in a smooth continuity, but as a valuable bequest'.[15] Calvert was a most willing beneficiary of this bequest. One can summarise the main influences on Calvert thus: Phelps provided the financial and commercial model, while Kean supplied the artistic, historical and literary template. Calvert combined these influences to form the basis of his own distinctive, innovative, spectacular, historically accurate yet financially successful Shakespearean revivals.

In 1856, Calvert was presented with the opportunity to act with Phelps's company and to experience the challenges of playing in provincial theatres. After the Surrey Theatre in Southwark had closed for the summer, he joined a small company that had been formed by members of Phelps's company to tour several provincial cities. Although the speculation was not financially successful, he concluded that 'the theatre of the provincial cities ... had been opened to them, and he had also gained in method and in finish by playing important parts with important actors'.[16] In 1859, he was offered his first employment as an actor-manager. The American actor and playwright Hermann Vezin wanted to lease the Surrey Theatre for the summer from the theatre's managers, William Creswick and Richard Shepherd. However, as a wealthy man, Vezin was concerned that the terms offered would be unfavourable, so he asked Calvert to obtain the theatre in his name and to be his stage manager.[17] (According to Iris Henson, 'in the nineteenth-century theatre the term "stage management" implied the organising and instructing of the actors in their roles and the overall control of such matters as setting and design; in other words it meant more or less what we mean nowadays by "direction".')[18] This tactic succeeded; Calvert managed the theatre for six weeks and opened there on 13 June 1859, playing the lead in *Macbeth*.

Experimentation and Adaptation: *Hamlet* and Melodrama

Eileen McCourt has recently argued that Phelps was attracted to those Shakespeare plays that had fallen out of the repertory, partly because he also needed an adventurous artistic policy to attract attention to suburban Islington.[19] But his commitment to legitimate theatre had a purpose wider than mere entertainment and financial success. McCourt believes that Phelps's purpose in management was also 'to inculcate appreciation of Shakespeare's words not necessarily with a pedagogic intent but to promote their appreciation through his interpretations'.[20] Creswick and Shepherd followed this model and endeavoured 'to do at the Surrey side what [Phelps] effected at the north end of the metropolis, by creating a taste for a better kind of amusement than that to which the people had become accustomed', and they were 'determined to ... raise the character of the house by providing an intellectual fare for its patrons'.[21]

John Knowles, the owner of Manchester's third Theatre Royal, which had opened in 1845, appointed Calvert as his actor-manager around September 1859 and, like Creswick and Shepherd, they jointly adopted as the template for their business model 'Mr. Phelps's conduct of Sadler's Wells Theatre'.[22] It is not known why

Knowles employed Calvert, since he left no correspondence or memoirs, but Calvert's experience at the Surrey Theatre would have made him the ideal person to introduce the best of Kean and Phelps to Knowles's establishment. As further evidence that both men were united in a desire to implement the best metropolitan practices, Knowles asked Calvert to 'go up' to London to see Phelps's production of the leading dramatist Tom Taylor's *The Fool's Revenge* and there 'make as many notes as you can, and jot down the colours and styles of the dresses, etc.'.[23]

Opening on 12 November 1859, Calvert's production of *Hamlet* provided him with an opportunity to apply what he had learned from Kean and Phelps and to demonstrate, at this early stage of his career in Manchester, his desire to achieve a realistic, historically accurate spectacle while turning a profit, supported by the modern infrastructure and robust business plan created by Knowles. He encountered some initial difficulties, however. According to his wife Adelaide, 'Shakespearean plays in the provinces were generally "pitchforked" on the stage. Any scenery and any costumes sufficed', and Calvert was 'indulging in the hope that he would be able to reform that altogether, and to give shape to some of his pet ideas'.[24] Although Knowles supported his ideas, he refused to spend any money on the scenery or costumes: 'there's lots of scenery in the cellar, and heaps of dresses in the wardrobe. Do whatever you like with them, but I shan't buy anything more.'[25] Calvert was thus forced to improvise. Knowles's resident scenic artist added representations of tapestries to the lower portions of scenery as makeshift representations of Norman interiors. Costumes were reused to achieve historical accuracy. Those made of satin and velvet used in previous productions of *Hamlet* were discarded and, in their place, 'an attempt was made at Scandinavian costumes by selecting only serges, cloths and clinging silks, the heavy woollen stockings being rolled over at the knees and cross-gartered – a thing not previously seen here'.[26]

The production was positively received; a review in one local newspaper boldly claimed that 'for the first time the play of *Hamlet* was historically truthful', and continued in the same supportive tone:

> The dresses and scenery were strictly accordant with the fashions prevailing in Denmark at the period to which the play supposed to refer. Hamlet is no longer the stale embodiment of stage usages and stage traditions. For the spangled velvet robe and plumed hat are substituted a close-fitting tunic of plain cloth of sober hue, and a simple cloak of like material, with a cap of similarly primitive and unpretending fashion. He now appears "in his habit as he lived".[27]

Even so, Knowles did not renew Calvert's contract after the summer of 1860. Possibly his involvement in the establishment of a project to build a new theatre, the Prince's Theatre, which opened in 1864, may have caused a conflict of interest.[28] Calvert became a journeyman actor-manager, being employed, for example, as stage-manager of Glasgow's Theatre Royal and Prince's Theatre concurrently from late 1862 until early 1863. He also continued to act and produce at Manchester's Theatre Royal, suggesting that there was apparently no enmity between the two men.[29] But the most distinctive feature of this phase of his career is his adaptation of existing melodramas, which he employed as prototypes from which he could assess the practicalities of creating texts suitable for his revivals.

In the nineteenth century French melodrama was extensively adapted and performed in Britain, as Carlotta Sorba has observed:

> As a new mixture of gestures, music and words, which spoke directly to the heart of men and women, the French genre of *melodrame* changed the theatrical experience of both popular and elite audiences. In England, the radical playwright Thomas Holcroft, a central figure in Anglo-French cultural exchanges, actively imported the French melodrama and helped to adapt it as a new theatrical genre to the specific English context.[30]

Kean commissioned melodramas for his theatre but, unlike Calvert, he did not adapt them himself. Alexandre Dumas *père*'s romantic novel *Les Frères Corses* (1845) had been adapted for the stage by Eugène Grangé and Xavier de Montépin, and premiered in Paris at Dumas' own Théâtre Historique on 10 August 1845. Kean admired this play and commissioned Dion Boucicault – for over three decades the most prolific playwright on the British stage - to write an adaptation; Boucicault's *The Corsican Brothers* opened at the Princess's on 24 February 1852, and won immediate success.[31]

To establish his reputation, Calvert needed to gain a foothold in provincial theatre, and he regarded melodrama as a suitable vehicle since, by the 1860s, touring companies had established the popularity of the genre outside London. Moreover, its universal appeal, adaptability and consequent earning potential made it a powerful medium through which theatre professionals and audiences could encounter Shakespeare for the first time. Marketing material such as advertisements and playbills promoted both current and future productions, so that audiences seeking a melodrama would simultaneously be made aware of a Shakespearean production. Melodrama also shared some characteristics with Calvert's later Shakespearean revivals. According to Rahill, melodrama 'is conventionally moral and humanitarian in point of view', which aligned with Calvert's religious beliefs, as demonstrated by his more ambivalent and less jingoistic version of *Henry V*.[32] Melodrama also 'offers elaborate scenic accessories and ... introduces music freely, typically to underscore dramatic effect'.[33] Calvert's revivals also employed extensive scenic elements, accompanied by music selected to create a mood in support of the action rather than to demonstrate any adherence to historical accuracy.

Calvert created his first adaptation while he was still in Knowles's employ, basing it on an American rather than a European play. This was *The Masked Mother; or, The Hidden Hand*,[34] by Emma Southworth, originally serialised in the *New York Ledger* between February and July 1859.[35] His next adaptation, which opened at Knowles's Theatre Royal in the first week of April 1861, was *The Island Home*, based on an obscure work, *La Dame de Saint-Tropez*, by the French dramatists Auguste Anicet-Bourgeois and Adolphe d'Ennery, first performed on 23 November 1844 at the Théâtre de la Porte-Saint-Martin in Paris. Calvert's version comprised four acts (the original being in five), with a licence for its performance at the Theatre Royal issued on 30 March 1861.[36] The play was set on the Caribbean island of Tortuga, an island of which Adam Blake was the sole proprietor; this concept of a man owning an island and being referred to as 'the God of this island' recalled *The Tempest*. This experimental work met with some success, with one reviewer insisting that 'we must speak in terms of praise of the manner in which it is put on the stage, and also of the very pleasant musical interspersed throughout'.[37] Anticipating Calvert's own desire to remove potentially offensive language from his Shakespearean revivals, the Lord Chamberlain's office stipulated that all oaths should be removed, including the phrase 'the God of this island'.[38]

Encouraged by the popularity and the positive reviews of his third adaptation, *Rube the Showman*, Calvert now moved away from adaptations and instead created an original melodrama in three acts; this was *The Hive of Life: Its Drones and Workers*, described as 'a play of "Now a days"',[39] (although one newspaper erroneously claimed that it too was adapted from the French).[40] The play was first mentioned in the *Era*: '*The Hive of Life* is in preparation and will shortly be produced with new scenery and dresses, Mr and Mrs C. Calvert take the leading characters'.[41] It was licensed by the Lord Chamberlain's Office on 7 June 1862 for performance in Glasgow.[42] It had, in fact, been first staged at the Queen's Theatre in Manchester on 21 April 1862, where it ran for five nights.[43] In the *Era* for 1 June 1862, Calvert took out an advertisement inviting theatre managers to engage him to produce this play, citing testimonials received from several Manchester newspapers.[44] From these periodicals, we discern that the play contained many of the features present in his Shakespearean revivals: high standards for scenery and costumes, and the dissemination of moral messages relevant to modern, industrialised cities. Indeed, the plot itself could have been a Shakespearean critique of those in power such as *The Tempest* or *Measure for Measure*; all the upper order are tyrants, the middle and lower classes are slaves and victims, and the lawyer is wily and unprincipled.[45] However, in the midst of general acclaim, the *Era* thought the subject matter too rich for its blood, stating that 'we do not admire the sentiment attempted to be conveyed, and happen to be of that class who believe that wickedness and fashionable vices are not indigenous to wealthy and aristocratic people ... and we should like to see Mr. Calvert devote his talents to a better and more healthy subject'.[46]

Calvert's final adaptation before his management of the Prince's Theatre commenced in 1864 was *The Duke's Signal*, based on the historical adventure novel *Le Bossu* (*The Hunchback*) by the French novelist and dramatist Paul Féval, first published in Paris in 1858. In it, Henri de Lagardère, a swashbuckling swordsman, disguises himself as a hunchback to avenge his friend, the Duke de Nevers, who has been murdered by Prince de Gonzague. A version titled *The Duke's Motto or I Am Here!* attributed to Féval and John Brougham, an English actor and dramatist, had opened at the Lyceum in London on 10 January 1863, and was first performed in Manchester at the Queen's Theatre on 20 May 1863, with Calvert as Lagardère and his wife, Adelaide, as Blanche.[47] The reception in the local press was positive: 'the piece has proved a great success, and the principal actors have nightly received that proof of public approval – a call before the curtain'.[48] Significantly, Calvert's version 'enjoyed over twenty revivals in various British and American cities over the next thirty years', a precursor to his international exports of *Richard III* and *Henry V*.[49] My research has not unearthed any copies of Calvert's acting editions of these adaptations. Perhaps he saw no commercial value in making them available to the public, nor is there any evidence that he sold the rights to his adaptations to other actors or managers.

Calvert's Acting Edition of *The Tempest*

From contemporary reviews, it seems that Calvert's adaptations were both critical and financial successes, which would have informed some of his artistic and commercial decisions when he produced his Shakespearean revivals at the Prince's Theatre. But why did he produce Shakespeare's plays at the Prince's Theatre at all, if these adaptations of melodramas were so successful? Although these adaptations were theatrically and commercially effective, they were not in any way historically instructive or educationally valuable and consequently they could not increase the prestige of the theatre by speaking of intellectuality or elite culture. To achieve this increased prestige, as Richard Schoch explains, theatrical historicism had to be applied not to 'quasi-historical melodramas, but to the national drama – i.e. to Shakespeare's authoritative account of English political history'.[50] In addition, Schoch argues that 'an historically accurate theatrical performance could succeed as history only if the dramatic action recovered an authentic moment of nation-building'. Such moments could not be found in Calvert's melodramas, but they could be found in Shakespeare.[51]

Acting editions were published play scripts, cut for performance and typically intended for use in productions in the amateur market or as reading copies, and often with lists of properties and set design sketches. They became popular in the profession in 1773, with *Bell's Shakespeare*, which was widely used for prompt-book-making for about three decades. Kemble's acting editions of the separate plays in his own repertoire were printed and reprinted from the 1790s until around 1815, and they generally displaced Bell for professional purposes. After the turn of the century, so-called standard acting editions proliferated: Mrs Inchbald's in about 1808, Oxberry's by 1820, Cumberland's about 1830, Hinds's *English Stage* in the late 1830s and Thomas Hailes Lacy's editions from the 1840s to about 1864. In the 1850s, Charles Kean revived Kemble's practice of publishing his own versions of the plays as he staged them, and after him Charles Calvert, Henry Irving and others followed suit.[52]

There are several reasons why Kean and Calvert produced their own acting editions. One reason is that they added status to a production and functioned as a form of advertising, like a modern-day theatre programme. All of Calvert's other editions were published in the same year as the revival, but *The Tempest* was a retrospective work. The list of revivals (in fact, only the first three of these are true revivals) quoted on its title page (Figure 1) comprises *Antony and Cleopatra* (1866), *A Midsummer Night's Dream* (1865), *Macbeth* (1866), *Much Ado About Nothing* (1865),

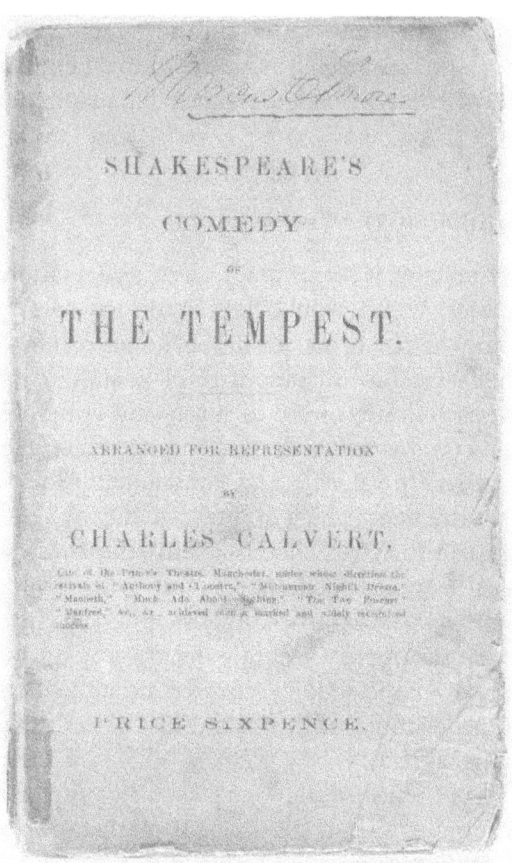

Figure 1 Title page of Charles Calvert's acting edition of *The Tempest* (1867/8). © University of Kent, supplied by Special Collections and Archives, University of Kent. All rights reserved.

The Two Foscari (1865) and *Manfred* (1867). As such, this edition was published after *Manfred* but before Calvert's next revival, *A Winter's Tale* in October 1868. Calvert himself is described as 'Late of the Prince's Theatre, Manchester', and if we interpret this as meaning 'no longer at', then this edition must have been published after his resignation from that theatre in June 1867, shortly before the end of his three-year contract. Calvert had become frustrated by the 'pin-pricks of annoyances' from the directors,[53] and wished 'to be his own master, free from the pound and pence supervision'.[54] Moreover, unlike his other acting editions, which state the theatre at which he was employed, this edition does not mention any theatre, so we can date it to that period during which he was not a manager, but was instead appearing as an actor in various northern towns and cities, that is, sometime between his resignation from the Prince's Theatre in June 1867 and his re-engagement at that same venue as manager in May 1868.

In October 1867, Calvert assisted Henry James Byron, the manager of Liverpool's Royal Alexandra Theatre on Lime Street, in a production of *The Tempest* which featured scenery by the Grieves, Calvert as Caliban, and 'a shipwreck ... managed more cleverly than anything previously seen in the town of this kind' featuring a moving mechanical ship.[55] Calvert had employed the Grieves as his scenic artists and had opened his revival in Manchester in October 1864 with a very similar shipwreck, so here is evidence that Calvert's influence extended beyond a mere acting role, anticipating his managerial partnership with Edward Saker's Shakespearean revivals at the same Liverpool theatre between 1876 and 1878. Perhaps Calvert commissioned a publicly available acting edition to support his tour (that it was available to the general public is proven by the price of sixpence being printed on the title page), while an examination of the list of scenes in an advertisement for Byron's revival shows it exactly matches the order of the scenes in the acting edition.[56] This revival achieved a long run, being produced for twenty-two nights at his Alexandra Theatre followed by five nights at the Royal Amphitheatre Theatre, also under his management.

Before analysing the text of Calvert's acting edition, I should offer some possible explanations for Calvert's choice of *The Tempest* for his first revival. The nineteenth-century development of spectacular revivals employing large numbers of actors, extensive properties and a multitude of scenic backdrops rendered frequent changes of setting impractical, since the time taken for each change would extend the length of the play and distract and frustrate the audience. For these reasons, Calvert was often forced into extensive reorganisations and consolidations of scenes. The third act of his *The Merchant of Venice* from 1871, for example, is formed of extracts from 1.2, 2.9, 2.1, 2.7 and 3.2. In *The Tempest*, however, the most complex and time-consuming scene to install on the stage is the first – the shipwreck – and Calvert was, therefore, not forced into significant reorganisations of subsequent acts. In his revival of the play, the opening scene depicted a storm and a wrecked ship which 'laboured so really in a tremendous sea as to bring almost a smell of salt water and its attendant incidents home to every spectator', Calvert having employed the local firm of John Byrnes to install mechanical apparatus to replicate the boat being tossed in the storm.[57] In this, Calvert followed Kean, who had employed a mechanical ship which required 'over 140 people to handle the machinery and a twenty-minute intermission after it was over to prepare for the next scene'.[58] A delay, for which Calvert's audiences would have been unprepared, ensued, since this apparatus needed to be moved from the stage and the setting for the next act installed, but later changes of setting involved less drastic movements of material, and so would have avoided testing the audience's patience and power of endurance. Indeed, the audience seems to have been forgiving of early teething troubles: 'the mechanical appliances of the stage, which are ample, and include the latest improvements of scenic art, were not worked with all the precision and skill that will come with use, and it was quite apparent that the audience understood and allowed for these slight drawbacks'.[59]

Although Calvert's acting edition was printed three years after he staged *The Tempest* in Manchester in 1864, we can be confident that the text is the one used for that earlier revival, principally because the text and order of scenes follow Kean's 1857 edition very closely, a cautious, derivative approach, as one might expect for a manager's first production at a new theatre whose reputation had not yet been established. Calvert's later texts are bolder and more innovative in their amendments, involving, for example, the insertion of tableaux depicting action that is not in Shakespeare's original text. The lack of scholarly embellishments in *The Tempest* also suggests it was used for the 1864 production. In all of Calvert's other acting editions, he followed Kean's lead by incorporating detailed historical notes. Kean's *The Tempest* opens with a five-page preface, three pages of 'Historical Notes to Act First', two pages of historical notes following the second act, one following the third act, three pages following the fourth act, and a single page to conclude the fifth act.[60] In his preface, Kean provided historical content by suggesting that *The Tempest* may have been inspired by the shipwreck of Sir George Somers on the Bermuda Islands in 1609, about three years before the production of the play. These islands were 'supposed to be enchanted by, and inhabited with witches and devils, which grew by reason of thunder-storm and tempest', and Kean himself speculated that 'this appalling visitation may, perhaps, have stimulated Shakespeare to compose a drama, which should combine a "topic of the day" with these wonders of far countries which were greedily received as facts by the credulous masses'.[61]

Historical notes are absent from Calvert's version of *The Tempest*, however. Even the introductory notes were not written by him, being reproduced *verbatim* from Samuel Taylor Coleridge's *Lectures on Shakespeare* (1811–19).[62] His later editions, in comparison, included extensive notes; his edition of *Henry V* (1872), for example, contains a lengthy contribution about heraldry written by Calvert's architect friend, Alfred Darbyshire.[63] These notes also included Calvert's rationale behind various aspects of his production, and comments about wider aspects of the theatre. His *Henry the Eighth* (1877) included an oblique reference to the second Lord Bishop of Manchester, James Fraser, who was the first clergyman in the world to preach in a theatre, expounding the virtues of Shakespeare as a means of purifying the theatre.[64]

An examination of Kean's edition shows that it is mostly a transcription of the First Folio with some text excised and rearranged (especially in the fifth act), but with few minor changes to the text retained and with even fewer additions to it: the most extensive changes were limited to updating the spelling throughout to reflect modern usage. Calvert, like Kean, wanted to use the most authentic text possible and, by doing so, preserve the essence of Shakespeare's plot and characterisations. It is therefore understandable that Calvert, in creating his own edition, followed Kean's text, even down to replicating the layout and font of the title page (Figure 2). Employing Kean's version as the basis of his own represents one mechanism by which Calvert imported the best of metropolitan theatre to Manchester, but he was determined to improve on it to achieve his vision of a spectacular, historically

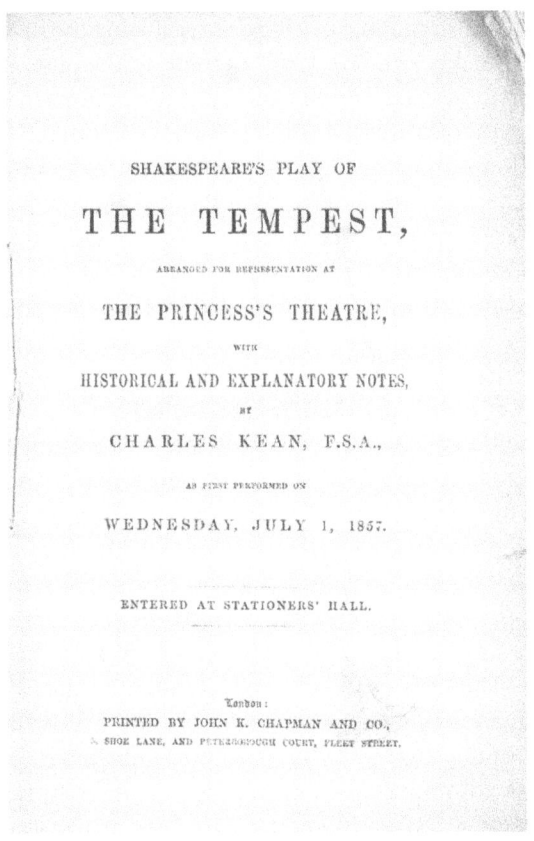

Figure 2 Title page of Charles Kean's acting edition of *The Tempest* (1857). Collection of the author. All rights reserved.

accurate and profitable one-nation Shakespeare; indeed, he was later described as 'a careful student of Shakespeare' whose acting editions were 'a pleasing memorial of his zeal and good sense'.[65] The very first scene, 1.1, immediately reveals an important divergence from Kean's edition. Kean completely excised the text from this scene, replacing it with the comments: 'the first scene, as now arranged, may be considered an introduction to the play; on its conclusion, therefore, the green curtain will descend, and the Overture will here be performed, for the purpose of giving time for the clearing away and re-setting of the stage'.[66] In contrast, Calvert reinstated most of the text for this scene directly from a Folio; Beddoes Peacock, deputy manager and treasurer at the Prince's Theatre from its opening, accompanied him to the Free Library at Heald Grove, where Professor Andrea Crestadoro, chief librarian of Manchester Free Libraries, placed at his disposal a 'treasure' so he could compare 'the acting edition with the folio edition sentence by sentence, so that it might be truly said the text had been faithfully followed'.[67] But which edition did he consult?

There were four Folios available in Manchester during the nineteenth century, of which three can be quickly rejected. Until its theft on the night of 12–13 July 1972, Manchester University owned a First Folio, but this had been donated in 1898 – almost two decades after Calvert's death – by Edward Donner (1840–1934), a local businessman and long-time member of the Council of Owens College and the University of Manchester.[68] In Manchester today, the John Rylands Library curates a First Folio but there is no evidence that this was ever located in the Free Library. Chetham's Library acquired a Third Folio in 1863, but there is no evidence of a connection between this establishment and Crestadoro. The Manchester Free Library, opened on 5 September 1852, was housed in the House of Science in Campfield prior to its move to its current location in St Peter's Square, opening as the Central Library on 17 July 1934. It is most likely, therefore, that Calvert consulted the Second Folio which is today located there. According to the library's catalogue, this Folio had been owned by the actor John Philip Kemble, who died on 26 February 1823, so the timeline for Calvert to have consulted it is correct.[69]

To achieve commercial success, Calvert needed to attract an audience composed of all sections of Manchester society, irrespective of social status, gender, race or religion, reflecting the city's increasingly cosmopolitan nature. He was, therefore, at pains to remove any language from his acting editions that might offend his potential audience. This was especially important in Manchester, since a host of religions had found a tolerant home there. According to Tristram Hunt, 'the most effective advocates of the Victorian city, of its ethos, its history and its values, were the Nonconformist communities', and among those communities, 'it was frequently the Unitarians ... who stood out as the most articulate champions of civic virtue'.[70] Even within Calvert's own circle of friends, there was a notable diversity of religious beliefs; Calvert was a Swedenborgian, Henry Irving was a Methodist, and Alfred Darbyshire was a Quaker.

In the first scene, Calvert regarded the word 'pox', present in the Folio and retained by Kean, as offensive because of its connotations of venereal diseases. Thus, 'A pox o' your throat, you bawling, blasphemous, incharitable dog!' (1.1.41–2) became 'A plague o' your throat, you bawling, blasphemous, incharitable dog!'; similarly, 'A pox o' your bottle!' (3.2.86) became 'A plague o' your bottle!' The idea of Sycorax's pregnancy was acceptable to Kean, who retained the Folio text, but not to Calvert, who changed 'this blue-eyed hag was hither brought with child,/And here was left by th' sailors' (1.1.322–3) to 'this blue-eyed hag was hither brought by the sailors'. Prospero's reference to Caliban's rape of Miranda was excised to preserve propriety: 'Filth as thou art, with humane care, and lodged thee/In mine own cell, till thou didst seek to violate/The honour of my child' (1.1.415–8) of the Folio and Kean's edition was amended to 'Filth as thou art, with humane care, and lodged thee/In mine own cell'. Prospero's words to Caliban – 'Thou poisonous slave, got by the devil himself/Upon thy wicked dam, come forth!' (1.2.384–5) – were modified by Calvert to remove any suggestion of diabolical rape: 'Thou poisonous slave, come forth!', where Kean was content to retain the Folio text.

Ferdinand's response, 'As I hope … Or night kept chained below' (4.1.33) contains the offensive line 'Mine honour into lust' (4.1.30); Calvert entirely removed this. He also removed descriptions of foul odours. When Trinculo meets Caliban in the fourth act, Calvert replaced 'Monster, I do smell all horse-pisse' (4.1.223–4) with 'Monster, I do smell most foully'. Even milder language relating to odours was culled: 'There, dancing up to th' chins, that the fowle Lake/O'er-stunck their feet' (4.1.204–5) was unacceptable to Calvert, and was discarded. Again, in his edition, Kean had reproduced the Folio text in full. Antonio's speech to Sebastian in the second act was excised, since it contained the words 'bosom' and 'molest':

> Ay, sir, where lies that? If 'twere a kibe,
> 'Twould put me to my slipper, but I feel not
> This deity in my bosom. Twenty consciences
> That stand 'twixt me and Milan, candied be they
> And melt ere they molest!
> (2.1.317–21)

Kean had removed only 'If 'twere a kibe,/'Twould put me to my slipper …' (2.1.317–8). Although Calvert restored most of the text of 1.1, which Kean had removed entirely, he deleted some dialogue containing the word 'wench': 'though the/ship were no stronger than a nutshell and as leaky/as an unstanched wench' (1.1.47–9). Calvert, like Kean, removed Miranda's words to Prospero containing the word 'womb': 'I should sin/To think but nobly of my grandmother./Good wombs have borne bad sons' (1.2.141–4). Like Kean, Calvert also excised an obscene part of Stephano's song: 'She loved not the savour of tar nor of pitch,/Yet a tailor might scratch her where'er she did itch' (2.2.53–4).

Calvert's reinstatement of the text of 1.1 also reintroduced one of the play's central motifs – a struggle between masters and servants – without which the play would lack one of its most important moral messages, an aspect of Shakespeare's works that he was keen to preserve to confer a greater measure of respectability on his revivals. The storm places everyone on the ship in mortal danger, and the usual relationships between them defined by class are disrupted. Boatswain's attempts to save the ship bring him into direct conflict with the nobles, who, despite their dependency on his efforts, are most annoyed at being rudely spoken to by a commoner. As the scene progresses, the characters speak less about the storm and more about the class conflict which undermines their attempts to survive it and to emphasise that this struggle is a class struggle, Shakespeare did not name the characters in the scene but instead referred to them by their role in society – Boatswain, Master, King and Prince. Without the text for 1.1, the audience would also have been deprived of the opportunity of realising, later in the play, the scene's inherent irony. Boatswain's observation on the insignificance of social hierarchies to natural phenomenon – 'What cares these roarers for the name of king?' (1.1.16–17) – is ironic, since neither the crew nor the audience are aware until later in the play that the storm is not natural at all, but is, in fact, a product of the self-appointed king of the island, Prospero.

Although Calvert followed most of the excisions that Kean had applied to the fifth act, he reversed all the rearrangements of the text that Kean had made, so that Calvert's text once again aligned with the Folio arrangement. Kean had moved the thirty lines of dialogue between Ariel, Boatswain, Alonso and Prospero – 'Sir, all this service ... Come hither, Spirit' (5.1.271–304) – to the end of Prospero's speech, preceding the entry of Ariel – 'Ye elves of hills and brooks ... I'll drown my book' (5.1.42–66). To directly follow this, Kean moved first the twelve lines of dialogue between Prospero, Ariel and Gonzalez – 'Why that's my dainty ... Out of this fearful country' (5.1.105–16) – and then Ariel's song, 'Where the bee sucks' (5.1.98–104). Calvert's rearrangements of passages of text are, in contrast, very minor. 'I will disease me, and myself present/As I was sometime Milan; dainty Spirit,/Thou shalt ere long be free' (5.1.95–7) is moved from immediately before 'where the bee sucks' (5.1.98–104) to after 'I'll drown my book'. (Note also a rare textual change here; he changed 'quickly spirit' to 'dainty spirit'.) Calvert transferred the Folio directions, 'Here enters Ariel before ...' (after 5.1.66 in the Folio) to before 'Where the bee sucks' (5.1.98–104). Finally, he moved 'Set Caliban and his companions free:/Untie the spell' (5.1.305–6) to follow 'not one of them/That yet looks on me, or would know me' (5.1.92–3).

Calvert's desire to preserve the original text as far as possible extended even to reversing minor modifications which Kean had applied, even though they would have had no impact on the action or the characterisations. Within the text, 'Come, thou tortoise' (1.2.379) was restored by Calvert; Kean had inserted 'forth' between 'Come' and 'thou'. Calvert retained 'By any other house or person?' (1.2.53), where Kean had changed 'house' to 'place'. Kean had changed Prospero's words to 'Sixteen years, Miranda, sixteen years since/Thy father was the Duke of Milan, and/A prince of power' (1.2.66–8); Calvert reinstated the original time period: 'Twelve year since, twelve year since'. Calvert restored 'O, if a virgin' (1.2.538) for Kean's 'O, if unmarried', and later 'No, as I am a man' (1.2.551) for Kean's 'No, as I am alive'. Similarly, Calvert rejected Kean's changes to Gonzalo's words – 'Are not, sir, my garments as fresh as the first day I wore them?' – in favour of the Folio's, 'Is not, sir, my doublet as fresh as the first day I wore it?' (2.1.107–8). He changed 'My child, they durst not' back to 'Dear, they durst not', thus reinstating the repetition of 'dear' with the next line, '('So dear the love my people bore me')' (1.2.168). This meticulous and uncompromising approach even extended to reinstating the Folio title of the play, *Shakespeare's Comedy of The Tempest*, which Kean had changed to *Shakespeare's Play of The Tempest*. Calvert trusted his audience to understand archaisms which Kean had often amended to reflect current language. For example, Kean had changed 'An undergoing stomach, to bear up/Against what should ensue' (1.2.187–8) to 'A courage to bear up/Against what should ensue'. Kean had similarly changed the words of Iris from 'And some donation freely to estate' to 'And some donation freely to bestow' (4.1.93). In both cases, Calvert reverted to the Folio version.

With an acting edition appropriate to the revival's artistic, spiritual and financial needs, Calvert had a firm basis on which to establish innovations in other aspects of the production. The playbill for his 1864 revival announced that five of the scenes had been painted by the Mancunian Frederick Holding, and three by the London-based Grieve family.[71] Thomas Grieve and his son Thomas Walford Grieve were mostly associated with their work in London, which had become the benchmark for excellence in scenery painting. Holding was better known for his watercolour paintings, but had contributed to Knowles's production of *Macbeth* at the Theatre Royal in 1854. It is important to note that Calvert commissioned new works from them, and did not simply transplant items from the capital. For the music, he innovated again, employing the music of a then-unknown composer, Arthur Sullivan, whose score had not even been composed for a play, but as a stand-alone graduation piece. In early 1863, Charles Hallé had included Sullivan's work, now extended to twelve movements, in two concerts in Manchester. Perhaps Calvert attended one of these concerts, or was made aware of Sullivan's work in some other way. In any event, Calvert's employment of his music was unusual, since the work had been created entirely from Sullivan's imagination instead of being commissioned by a theatre manager for a specific production. The music arranger was another recruit from London, Ferdinand Wallerstein, until recently the leader of the St James's Theatre. Throughout his revivals, Calvert demonstrated an eclectic approach to his choice of music, which apparently contravened his customary insistence on historical accuracy. However, Calvert's aim was to create a mood by selecting musical extracts of a variety of genres typical of a location or era. For *The Tempest*, Sullivan's score was supplemented by extracts from Arne and Purcell.[72]

With the highest quality scenery and suitable music to complement his acting edition, staged within a theatre whose capacity was able to generate profitable revenue, Calvert's revival was an artistic, critical and commercial success, delivering financial stability to the Prince's Theatre despite the severe local economic difficulties prevailing at the time. Beddoes Peacock later recalled that the success of *The Tempest* was achieved despite 'Lancashire ... going through the throes of a cotton famine', caused by overproduction in a time of contracting world markets and by the blockading of the southern American ports during the Civil War which interrupted cotton imports.[73] The situation was aggravated by cotton workers in Manchester who, at a meeting on 31 December 1862, decided to boycott American cotton in support of Abraham Lincoln and the anti-slavery faction, despite their own consequent impoverishment. In spite of these challenges, *The Tempest* was performed thirty-one times in 1864 with a total attendance of 62,000, and was repeated the following Easter with a further fourteen performances, achieving, for the first time in Manchester, long runs which became not just a feature of Calvert's revivals but a necessity for their commercial success.[74]

Calvert's production of *The Tempest* provided a template for the attainment of artistic and financial success that he was able to apply to his later revivals, not just in Manchester but across the globe. Towards the end of 1874, in an effort to salvage a financially disastrous season at their Booth's Theatre in New York, Henry Jarrett and Henry Palmer made the directors of the Prince's Theatre a 'liberal offer' for Calvert's *Henry V*.[75] This most English of plays presenting the most English of kings may not at first sight have appeared to be a likely success in America, but Calvert's *Henry V* proved to be the ideal production, since his version – despite employing spectacular settings and tableaux – was 'no indulgent, thoughtless escape into jingoism, but a judicious blend of rejoicing and sorrow'.[76] His acting edition incorporated the ambivalence of the play's presentation of war by reinstating the often-deleted incidents that challenged the heroic portrayal of Henry: the massacre of the French prisoners after Agincourt, the threats to destroy Harfleur and the execution of Bardolph. This export contributed to the lead actor, Birmingham's George Rignold, becoming the first global Shakespearean celebrity, as he reprised his role as Henry across the United States, Canada and Australasia using variants of Calvert's original acting edition, performed among replicas of Calvert's costumes, scenery and properties.

Thus, through his revivals, Calvert revealed the potential of Shakespeare's cultural value in the commercial and religious as well as artistic arenas, and created a one-nation Shakespearean theatrical commodity with universal appeal which even generated demand from overseas, despite him having no global ambitions of his own.

Notes

The source of the original Folio text and associated line numbering throughout is William Shakespeare, *The Tempest*, eds Barbara A. Mowat and Paul Werstine, with Michael Poston and Rebecca Niles (Folger Shakespeare Library): https://folger-main-site-assets.s3.amazonaws.com/uploads/2022/11/the-tempest_PDF_FolgerShakespeare.pdf [accessed 16 February 2025].

Manchester's Central Library curates an archive of correspondence sent to Andrea Crestadoro, some of which includes letters from Charles Calvert. These letters demonstrate his desire to ascertain the finest details about building and settings. As well as curating the only known bound copy of the acting editions of Calvert's revivals (except *The Tempest*), the John Rylands Library holds the archive of his friend, Alfred Darbyshire. This contains the finest collection of ephemera relating to the revivals including playbills, programmes, letters from famous actors such as Henry Irving, and artefacts relating to Calvert's funeral.

1 *North London Record* (29 October 1864), p. 3.
2 *Daily News* (London), (17 October 1864), p. 2.
3 Richard Foulkes, *The Calverts: Actors of Some Importance* (London: The Society for Theatre Research, 1992), p. 118.
4 George C. D. Odell, *From Betterton to Irving*, vol. 2 (New York: Charles Scribner's Sons, 1920), p. 358.
5 Leigh Hunt, *Critical Essays on the Performers of the London Theatres* (London: John Hunt, 1807), appendix, p. 31.
6 *Theatrical Examiner* (23 July 1815), p. 2.

7 Richard W. Schoch, *Shakespeare's Victorian Stage: Performing History in the Theatre of Charles Kean* (Cambridge: Cambridge University Press, 1998), p. 15.
8 J. C. Trewin, *Mr. Macready: A Nineteenth-Century Tragedian and His Theatre* (London: Harrap, 1955), p. 148.
9 Shirley S. Allen, *Samuel Phelps and Sadler's Wells Theatre* (Middletown, CT: Wesleyan University Press, 1971), pp. 40–1.
10 Adrian Poole, *Shakespeare and the Victorians* (London: Arden Shakespeare, 2004), p. 204.
11 Michael. R. Booth, *Theatre in the Victorian Age* (Cambridge: Cambridge University Press, 1991), pp. 48–9.
12 Russell Jackson, *Victorian Theatre: A New Mermaid Background Book* (London: A. & C. Black, 1989), pp. 260–1.
13 *Ibid.*
14 John Coleman, *Fifty Years of an Actor's Life*, vol. 1 (London: Hutchinson & Co, 1904), pp. 113–14.
15 Booth, *Theatre in the Victorian Age*, p. 47.
16 Adelaide Calvert, *Sixty-Eight Years on the Stage* (London: Mills & Boon, 1911), pp. 48–9.
17 *Ibid.*, p. 50.
18 Iris Henson, 'The Stage Manager Then and Now', *Theatre Notebook*, 42:3 (1988), 99.
19 Eileen M. C. McCourt, 'Samuel Phelps at Sadler's Wells Theatre, 1844–1862' (PhD thesis, University of Birmingham, 2019), p. 116.
20 *Ibid.*, p. 196.
21 William Creswick, *An Autobiography: A Record of Fifty Years of the Professional Life of the Late William Creswick* (London: James Henderson, 1889), p. 70.
22 *Ibid.*
23 Calvert, *Sixty-Eight Years*, p. 60.
24 *Ibid.*, pp. 58–9.
25 *Ibid.*
26 *Ibid.*, pp. 59–60.
27 *Manchester Courier and Local General Advertiser* (19 November 1859), p. 10.
28 Calvert, *Sixty-Eight Years*, p. 63.
29 Foulkes, *Calverts*, p. 40.
30 Carlotta Sorba, 'Melodrama in Post-Revolutionary Europe: The Genealogy and Diffusion of a "Popular" Theatrical Genre and Experience, 1780–1830', in Peter Borsay and Jan Hein Furnée (eds), *Leisure Cultures in Urban Europe, c.1700–1870: A Transnational Perspective* (Manchester: Manchester University Press, 2016), p. 50.
31 James L. Smith, *Victorian Melodramas* (London: J. M. Dent & Sons Ltd, 1976), p. 142.
32 Frank Rahill, *The World of Melodrama* (University Park: Pennsylvania State University Press, 1967), p. xiv, quoted in Carolyn Williams (ed.), *The Cambridge Companion to English Melodrama* (Cambridge: Cambridge University Press, 2018), p. 1.
33 *Ibid.*
34 Allardyce Nicoll, *A History of English Drama 1660–1900. vol. 5: Late Nineteenth Century Drama 1850–1900* (Cambridge: Cambridge University Press, 1946), p. 783.

35 Marie Léger-St-Jean, 'Price One Penny: A Database of Cheap Literature, 1837–1860': http://www.priceonepenny.info [accessed 21 February 2024].
36 Royal Holloway University of London, 'Lord Chamberlain's Plays, 1852–1866. Plays licensed in 1861': https://intranet.royalholloway.ac.uk/dramaandtheatre/documents/pdf/lcp/playslicensedin1861.pdf [accessed 10 June 2024], p. 5.
37 *Era* (7 April 1861), p. 13.
38 Royal Holloway University of London, 'Lord Chamberlain's Plays, 1852–1866. Plays licensed in 1861', p. 5.
39 Royal Holloway University of London, 'Lord Chamberlain's Plays, 1852–1866. Plays licensed in 1862': https://intranet.royalholloway.ac.uk/dramaandtheatre/documents/pdf/lcp/playslicensedin1862.pdf [accessed 10 June 2024], p. 9.
40 *Dublin Evening Mail* (24 April 1863), p. 3.
41 *Era* (30 March 1862), p. 12.
42 Lord Chamberlain's Plays, 1852–1866. Plays licensed in 1862, p. 9.
43 *Manchester Courier and Local General Advertiser* (26 April 1862), p. 6.
44 *Era* (1 June 1862), p. 16.
45 *Dublin Evening Mail* (24 April 1863), p. 3.
46 *Era* (13 September 1863), p. 12.
47 Royal Holloway University of London, 'Lord Chamberlain's Plays, 1852–1866. Plays licensed in 1863': https://intranet.royalholloway.ac.uk/dramaandtheatre/documents/pdf/lcp/playslicensedin1863.pdf [accessed 10 June 2024], p. 12.
48 *London Evening Standard* (5 January 1863), p. 1.
49 Russell Jackson, 'Victorian and Edwardian Stagecraft: Techniques and Issues', in Kerry Powell (ed.), *The Cambridge Companion to Victorian and Edwardian Theatre* (Cambridge: Cambridge University Press, 2004), p. 84.
50 Schoch, *Shakespeare's Victorian Stage*, p. 10.
51 *Ibid.*
52 Charles Harlen Shattuck, *The Shakespeare Promptbooks: A Descriptive Catalogue* (Urbana: University of Illinois Press, 1965), p. 8.
53 Calvert, *Sixty-Eight Years*, p. 83.
54 *Ibid.*, p. 84.
55 *Manchester Courier and Local General Advertiser* (30 October 1867), p. 4.
56 *Liverpool Daily Post* (22 October 1867), p. 4.
57 *Manchester Times* (22 October 1864), p. 6.
58 Virginia M. Vaughan, *Shakespeare in Performance: 'The Tempest'* (Manchester: Manchester University Press, 2011), p. 41.
59 *Manchester Times* (22 October 1864), p. 6.
60 Charles Kean (ed.), *Shakespeare's Play of The Tempest Arranged for Representation at the Princess's Theatre with Historical and Explanatory Notes* (London: John K. Chapman and Co., 1857), pp. [v]–ix, 27–9, 41–2, 52, 62–4, 74.
61 *Ibid.*, pp. vi–vii.
62 Samuel Taylor Coleridge, 'Lecture 1: Thursday, 17 December 1818 (*The Tempest*)', in Adam Roberts (ed.), *Coleridge: Lectures on Shakespeare (1811–1819)* (Edinburgh University Press, 2016), pp. 132–40.

63 Charles Calvert (ed.), *Shakspere's Historical Play of Henry the Fifth: Arranged for Representation in Five Acts* (Manchester: Henry Blacklock & Co., 1872), pp. 78–80.
64 Charles Calvert (ed.), *Henry the Eighth by William Shakespeare: Arranged for Representation from the Text by Charles Calvert and First Produced at the Theatre Royal, Manchester* (London: W. S. Johnson, Nassau Steam Press, 1877), p. iii.
65 A. W. Ward, *The Dictionary of National Biography*, entry for Charles Calvert quoted in Foulkes, *Calverts*, p. 57.
66 Kean, *The Tempest*, p. 11.
67 Manchester, Manchester Central Library, *Material Relating to Charles Calvert*, Th792.094273Ca2 (cutting annotated as being from *Manchester City News*, June 1879). This cutting was referred to by Foulkes, *Calverts*, p. 57, as 'details from an unidentified news cutting in the Local History Library, Manchester Central Library'.
68 James Peters, 'The Theft of the First Folio, 1972': https://rylandscollections.com/2022/07/13/the-theft-of-the-first-folio-1972/ [accessed 6 May 2024].
69 Robert Allot (ed.), *Mr. William Shakespeare's comedies, histories and tragedies* [second folio], (n.p., Thomas Cotes, 1632?).
70 Tristram Hunt, *Building Jerusalem: The Rise and Fall of the Victorian City* (London: Weidenfeld & Nicolson, 2004), p. 141.
71 Matthew Lloyd, 'Arthur Lloyd's Music Hall and Theatre History Website', *The Prince's Theatre, Oxford Street, Manchester*: www.arthurlloyd.co.uk/ManchesterTheatres/PrincessTheatreManchester.htm [accessed 11 June 2024].
72 *Daily News* (London) (17 October 1864), p. 2.
73 Manchester, Manchester Central Library, *Material Relating to Charles Calvert*, Th792.094273Ca2 (cutting annotated as being from *Manchester City News*, June 1879). This cutting was referred to by Foulkes, *Calverts*, p. 57, as 'details from an unidentified news cutting in the Local History Library, Manchester Central Library'.
74 *Era* (14 June 1884), p. 8.
75 Calvert, *Sixty-Eight Years*, p. 146.
76 Richard Foulkes, 'Charles Calvert's *Henry V*', *Shakespeare Survey*, 41:29 (1989), 32.

Religious Revival and the Challenge of Evangelical Primitivism: Opposition to the Brethren and Lay Preachers in Ulster after the 1859 Revival

ANDREW R. HOLMES,
QUEEN'S UNIVERSITY, BELFAST

Abstract
Although the Irish origins of the Brethren are well known, scholars have paid little attention to the growth and impact of this form of evangelical primitivism in Ireland. This article addresses that issue by considering opposition to the Brethren and lay preachers in Ulster after the 1859 revival. It shows how criticism was stimulated by the numerical growth of the Brethren, embarrassment at the religious populism unleashed during 1859 and the perception that the Brethren posed a threat to protestant unity. It considers the critique of the Brethren offered by members of the regionally dominant Presbyterian Church in Ireland, and what their criticisms tells us about the relationships between revivalism and denominations, as well as the subsequent development of the Brethren and popular evangelicalism in Northern Ireland after 1921.

Keywords: Brethren; revivalism; evangelicalism; Ireland; Ulster

The religious revivals that marked the expansion of evangelicalism from the 1780s had a significant effect on protestants across the North Atlantic world. These outbreaks of religious fervour challenged traditional understandings of authority and church organisation by promoting itinerant preaching, voluntary religious associations and lay agency.[1] In the United States, Christianity was democratised as ordinary women and men were empowered through, for instance, black churches, the Disciples of Christ, Methodism and Mormonism.[2] Even though the United Kingdom had protestant state churches, this evangelical surge also led to the growth of alternative denominations, especially Methodism, and the emergence of new forms of Christianity. An example of this process was the Christian Brethren, popularly known as the Plymouth Brethren, a label that may be applied to a variety of fellowships and individuals that emerged from the 1820s. The 'deepest, most basic doctrine' of the Brethren 'was an unwavering belief in the depiction in the New Testament of the primitive church'.[3] It was a form of protestant primitivism that sought to return to the simplicity of the New Testament, and to separate from worldliness and error. It asserted the infallibility and sole authority of the Bible, celebrated weekly communion and rejected formal church structures, including an ordained clergy and denominational labels. The Brethren also held a pessimistic view of the End Times that eventually developed into dispensational premillennialism. Donald Akenson has demonstrated how this collection of ideas and practices was transported from its origins in Ireland and Britain to the United States, where it was inculturated as a key component of the evangelicalism embraced by many white Americans in the twentieth century.[4] Though never numerically dominant, the Brethren exercised a significant influence on global evangelicalism by popularising dispensationalism and extending the practice of so-called 'faith missions' that bypassed traditional missionary societies. According to David Bebbington, the Brethren were 'radical, intense, quixotic', and 'played a distinctive role as evangelicals of the evangelicals'.[5]

Despite their influence, the small numerical size of the Brethren is a reminder that they were more likely to attract criticism than adherents. Indeed, the significance of the criticisms published in the second half of the nineteenth century inspired F. R. Coad, one of the first modern chroniclers of the movement, 'to correct the perspective engendered by those writings of the past'.[6] Tim Grass, in his invaluable study of the Open Brethren, has noted that these criticisms of the movement were wide ranging and included charges of theological error, overturning church order, engaging in proselytism, promoting schism, displaying spiritual pride, flouting the perpetual obligation of the moral law and holding a faulty understanding of Christian experience.[7] Grass points out that the 'most vehemently critical works came from Presbyterians', and these critics, as this article shows, were often to be found in Ireland.[8] Coad and Grass also suggest that the ferocity of criticism explains the greater rigidity and separatism of the movement in twentieth-century Northern Ireland.[9] The Irish context is also vital in explaining the origins of the Brethren. Their emergence can be traced to the formidable challenges faced by the state Church of Ireland in the 1820s, most obviously that it was the church of a protestant minority, and to John Nelson Darby, a curate in that church who would become the most famous Brethren leader.[10] Aside from these origins in the south of Ireland and the pioneering work of Tim Grass, historians of religion have paid little attention to the development of the Brethren even in the northern province of Ulster, the only one of the four Irish provinces that contained a protestant majority.[11]

This article charts the numerical growth of the Brethren in Ulster after the revival of 1859 and explores why this alarmed Presbyterians, the dominant protestant church in the north of Ireland. It demonstrates that criticism was stimulated by embarrassment at the religious populism unleashed during that 'Year of Grace' and its equivocal legacy, including the threat that it posed to protestant unity against a Catholic population that was growing in political self-confidence. The revival also prompted a change in the character and social profile of the Brethren. Originally associated with well-educated but disillusioned young men of independent means within the southern Irish Anglican elite, the movement that the critics met in the north-eastern counties was often led by lay itinerant preachers from humble backgrounds. Yet in order to respond to the Brethren threat, critics had to rely on the publications of sophisticated writers such as Darby and C. H. Mackintosh to define the doctrine and organisation even of Brethren who rejected Darby's views. As a consequence, Grass notes that their criticisms did not always do justice to the variety of views held by the various Brethren groups.[12] The article begins by examining the origins of the Brethren in Ireland, the ambiguous legacy of the 1859 revival, and the numerical growth of the movement in Ulster between 1861 and 1911. The following two sections consider the Presbyterian critique of the Brethren in Ulster during the same period. The article concludes with reflections on what the Presbyterian response tells us about the relationships between revivalism and denominations, as well as the subsequent development of the Brethren and popular evangelicalism in Northern Ireland after 1921.

Origins, Revival and Numerical Growth

The Irish origins of the Brethren are well known. The primitivist impulse that the Brethren embodied was a product of the challenges faced by the Church of Ireland in the early nineteenth century.[13] Although it was the state church since the sixteenth century, and the church of the landed elite who dominated political and social life, it was the church of an Episcopalian minority. Catholics comprised over three-quarters of the Irish population, and in protestant Ulster the largest protestant community was Presbyterian. The Act of Union that created the United Kingdom of Great Britain and Ireland in January 1801 incorporated Ireland into a parliamentary union, and the Irish church into 'The United Church of England and Ireland'. Despite significant state support in the first two decades of the century, the minority Church of Ireland came to be seen as an obstacle to reconciling the Catholic majority to the union state. As a consequence, the Catholic Relief Act of 1829 permitted Catholics to become members of the Westminster parliament, and the structures and finances of the Church of Ireland were streamlined by the Church Temporalities Act (1833) and the Tithe Rentcharge (Ireland) Act (1838).

For many within the United Church, these measures challenged its spiritual independence and amounted to Erastianism. In response, many turned to the Bible for guidance on the simplicity of the Early Church and to place their difficulties within prophetic time.[14] Especially important were those connected with Trinity College, Dublin, such as Anthony Norris Groves, Edward Cronin and John Gifford Bellett, who met together in their homes and celebrated communion without recourse to clergy or liturgy. They were joined by John Nelson Darby, a curate in the Church of Ireland, who began to formulate a theology of 'the ruin of the church' that abandoned the idea of state churches, and their dissenting alternatives, and sought a return to the primitive simplicity of the New Testament. From that insight, Darby developed a pessimistic form of premillennialism, which saw the true church of believers as an embattled remnant and the Earth descending into spiritual chaos before the Second Coming of Christ.[15]

Darby grew estranged from the state church and joined with others, such as George Muller and Benjamin Willis Newton, in a religious network sustained by fellowship groups, correspondence and itinerancy. One of the reasons for the success of this network was that it attracted individuals from a similar background: 'young, well-bred, well-educated and well-travelled new Evangelicals'.[16] Yet there was always the possibility of schism owing to the tension between open fellowship and separatism. This was exacerbated by personalities, and the movement split at Plymouth in 1848 when Darby's denunciation of Newton led to the formation of Open and Exclusive varieties, the latter of which was dominated by Darby and would remain the largest Brethren grouping at the end of the nineteenth century. The Open Brethren began to expand throughout the United Kingdom from the late 1850s in response to religious revival in general as well as their own efforts.[17] Open assemblies began to proliferate from the 1860s, especially in south-west England, parts of Scotland and Ulster. This growth changed the social profile of the Brethren, as the membership became more working class and their religiosity more populist. According to Neil Dickson, 'after 1859 the movement to some extent was remade, with Brethrenism inheriting not only the anti-establishment spirit of mid-century revivalism, but also its lay orientation'.[18] Tensions between the clergy and the laity during and after the revivals of the late 1850s stimulated Brethren growth. Their own understanding of the church emphasised 'the priesthood of all believers, liberty of ministry, diversity of gifts and the sovereignty of the Spirit', yet the potential liberty that this suggested for the laity was offset by a social and political conservatism that significantly restricted the role of women.[19]

Ulster played a central role in the transatlantic revivals of the late 1850s that began in the eastern United States in 1857. In the summer of 1859, the province experienced a revival that would become the religious golden age for subsequent generations of Ulster Protestants.[20] Supporters claimed that around 100,000 individuals were converted, churches and individual believers reinvigorated, and public and personal morality improved. The Presbyterian Church in Ireland had been preparing the ground for a revival since the 1830s, and Presbyterian spokesmen became the revival's foremost apologists, most notably William Gibson, who in 1860 published *The Year of Grace* in response to requests from evangelicals in the United States.[21] Yet the events of 1859 differed from the sober revival envisaged by the clerical elite, and it unleashed a religious populism that was difficult to control.[22] Some conversions were accompanied by unprecedented physical manifestations, most notably individuals being 'struck down', and by various other signs and wonders. The religious experience of converts was so intense that many claimed instantaneous conversion and assurance of salvation, both of which were frowned upon by some confessional Calvinists. Furthermore, the revival stimulated lay preaching. The official 'State of Religion' report submitted to the General Assembly of the Presbyterian Church in Ireland in June 1859 acknowledged that the 'work has been carried forward in many districts by the agency of the converts themselves'. The report noted that many of these were 'uneducated persons, of humble station', who, 'without embarrassment or trepidation', prayed and preached the gospel in public.[23]

Presbyterian ministers who supported the revival sought to downplay these features, but it was difficult to ignore the growth of smaller evangelical groups who had a populist appeal. For the rest of the century, the Presbyterian Church sought to harness the power of evangelical populism unleashed in 1859 for denominational ends. Aspects of popular revivalism, including the extension of lay agency, were adopted, and there was widespread support for the revivalism of D. L. Moody.[24] What made things difficult for Presbyterian writers was that they could not dismiss out of hand the activities and success of their fellow evangelicals, including those sympathetic to the Brethren. For instance, Henry Grattan Guinness, a well-known evangelist associated with the Brethren, was active in Ulster during 1859. Guinness published an account of the revival compiled of letters from his acquaintances in the province, most of whom were Presbyterians, including the Clerk of the General Assembly.[25] C. H. Mackintosh, one of Darby's lieutenants in the Exclusive Brethren, twice visited areas affected by the revival in Mid Antrim and east Londonderry. In keeping with the Brethren rejection of denominational labels, Mackintosh advised the readers of *Things New and Old* to 'carefully guard against eyeing this movement as a means of subserving the interests of *a party*'.[26] He went on, 'we claim for ourselves, and we cede to others, the privilege of worshipping God according to the light which He may impart; but we would rather be the honoured instrument in bringing one soul into the fold of Christ, than to conduct ten thousand into any denominational enclosure'.[27]

Such proclamations of gospel disinterestedness were viewed with suspicion by evangelicals in other denominations. William Crook, a Methodist minister in Sligo, addressed such claims in a pamphlet published in 1865. Crook noted that under the 'pretext' of simply spreading the Gospel, Mackintosh and numerous lay preachers had 'wormed' their way into revival districts. They had 'leavened the popular mind in Ulster with the new Gospel of the Darbyites and Plymouth brethren', through preaching and hundreds of 'handbills, placards, and Darbyite pamphlets'. Crook claimed that the results were catastrophic. The 'peace and unity of many families were broken up', hypocritical believers proclaimed their 'resurrection life' but 'were dead in trespasses and in sins', and the precepts of the moral law were set aside owing to a misunderstanding of the biblical injunction that they were under grace and not the law.[28]

Much of Crook's information was drawn from the writings of J. C. L. Carson, a Baptist physician in Coleraine. Carson had written pamphlets vindicating the scriptural character of the 1859 revival, but his name is most associated with the many editions of *The Heresies of the Plymouth Brethren*. The Brethren historian Roy Coad wrote that Carson 'adopted a number of hobby-horses, which he rode with vigour', and that although the 'book makes amusing reading for the idler today ... in its day it was vicious'.[29] Carson's work was first published in 1862, and had originally appeared as a series of letters to a local newspaper, the *Coleraine Chronicle*, the first of which focused on what he saw as Mackintosh's heretical views on the divinity and humanity of Christ.[30] Carson dismissed from the outset the claim that the Brethren had no system of theology; rather, they had 'a very complete system', and were 'as tyrannical as Rome in keeping their followers to it'.[31] In order to make his case, Carson focused on the Exclusive branch of the movement, especially Mackintosh and Darby, and ignored those representing other strands of Brethrenism. Carson admitted it would be 'impossible to manage such wily and slippery customers' unless the critic was properly versed in the opinions of the Brethren, adhered strictly to the Bible, and argued with precision and tenacity. In the beginning, the aims of the movement were good, and it was associated with 'many excellent men', but it had 'now run into the wildest extremes imaginable; has become as entirely Jesuitical as the system of Loyola itself; and by the denial of the moral law as the rule of life, has led, in many instances, to the most disastrous consequences'.[32]

That a Baptist writer felt so strongly about the growth of the Brethren indicates that both groups were vying to exploit the religious upsurge of the 1859 revival. The Baptists were enthusiastic in their support for the revival, yet it was a mixed blessing for them. For instance, the congregation in Derry was formed in 1860, but soon folded as many left to join the Brethren. Baptist growth in general was held back by 'the disorganizing influence of the Plymouth Brethren', with whom they shared much in common, including the rejection, at that point, of a separate pastoral office and the practice of adult baptism by the Open Brethren.[33] The most sensational case of an individual moving from the Baptists to the Brethren was John Galway McVicker.[34] McVicker already had a previous career as a minister with the Eastern Reformed Presbyterian Synod of Ireland, and was converted during the 1859 revival. McVicker underwent believers' baptism in September by Jeremiah Meneely, a layman and one of the first converts of the revival. Even though he had previously rejected adult baptism, McVicker became the pastor of a Baptist fellowship in Ballymena. On 13 December 1862, the *Ballymena Observer* announced that an 'unexpected vacancy' had occurred in that congregation: McVicker had resigned 'and united himself with a religious body commonly called "the Plymouth Brethren," the tenets of which are but little known among the community of this neighbourhood'.[35] The *Observer*'s claim that a religious society being formed by McVicker in High Street held the principles of the Plymouth Brethren was rejected by its members, who claimed that they were 'not connected, nor intended to be connected, with that body, nor with any other religious society on the face of the earth'.[36]

The numerical growth of the Brethren and other evangelical groups after the 1859 revival can be traced through Irish census records, which, unlike British censuses, included a question about religious affiliation. Between 1861 and 1911, the two largest protestant churches in Ulster – the Presbyterian Church in Ireland and the Church of Ireland – declined in absolute numbers as the provincial population fell by 332,540, though they continued to represent around 27% and 23% of the provincial population respectively. During the same period, Methodist numbers grew from 32,030 to 48,816, representing an increase of the population share from 1.7% to 3.1%. Similarly, those in the 'all other denominations' category

Table 1
Total number of self-described adherents of the four largest Brethren groups in Ulster, 1861–1911

	1861	1871	1881	1891	1901	1911
Christian Brethren	131	999	1,189	1,389	2,036	2,554
Christians	38	529	1,313	2,716	2,192	1,900
Brethren	26	120	947	1,238	2,478	4,300
Plymouth Brethren	13	269	401	526	850	1,364
Total	208	1,917	3,850	5,869	7,556	10,118

Source: Census of Ireland for the Year 1861. Part IV. Reports and Tables Relating to Religious Professions, Education, and Occupations. Volume. II. Religions and Occupations (Dublin, 1863), 483; Census of Ireland, 1871. Part I. Area, Houses, and Population: Also the Ages, Civil Condition, Occupations, Birthplaces, Religion, and Education of the People. Vol. III. Province of Ulster (Dublin, 1875), 1044; Census of Ireland, 1881. Part I. Area, Houses, and Population: Also the Ages, Civil or Conjugal Condition, Occupations, Birthplaces, Religion, and Education of the People. Vol. III. Province of Ulster (Dublin, 1882), 994; Census of Ireland, 1891. Part I. Area, Houses, and Population: Also the Ages, Civil or Conjugal Condition, Occupations, Birthplaces, Religion, and Education of the People. Vol. III. Province of Ulster. Summary Tables and Indexes (Dublin, 1892), 994; Census of Ireland, 1901. Part I. Area, Houses, and Population: Also the Ages, Civil or Conjugal Condition, Occupations, Birthplaces, Religion, and Education of the People. Vol. III. Province of Ulster. Summary Tables (Dublin, 1902), 31; Census of Ireland, 1911. Area, Houses, and Population: Also the Ages, Civil or Conjugal Condition, Occupations, Birthplaces, Religion, and Education of the People. Province of Ulster. Summary Tables (Dublin, 1912), 37.

rose from 20,443 to 53,881, and as a proportion of the overall provincial population from 1.1% to 3.4%.[37] For Nicola Morris, the growth of Methodism represented the continued and growing significance of evangelicalism in Ulster, and this conclusion is supported by the fact that the bulk of the 'others' were decidedly evangelical in outlook and were associated with Congregationalists, Baptists, the Salvation Army and, of course, the Brethren.[38] Although they shunned denominational labels, the Brethren had to describe themselves as something, and, in the main, they adopted one of four labels – Christian Brethren, Christians, Brethren, and Plymouth Brethren. Less common self-descriptors included Darbyites, Open and Exclusive Brethren, Brethren in Christ, and 'Christians meeting in the name of Jesus Christ'. Taken together, the four principal descriptors comprised the lion's share of the Brethren cohort, and demonstrate its growing numerical existence after 1859 (Table 1).

As the cohort grew, the terms 'Christian Brethren' and 'Christian' became less popular in comparison to the general 'Brethren' label, and this may reflect a growing sense of denominational distinctiveness. More generally, the fact that the Brethren movement was growing as a result of the 1859 revival, and was difficult even to label, suggests why it faced such opposition from the largest protestant church in the province.

Criticism During the 1860s

Presbyterians were worried about the growth of smaller evangelical groups in the decades after 1859. In May 1861, the Synod of Ballymena and Coleraine, which covered the heartland of the 1859 revival, met to consider their annual report on the State of Religion.[39] Resolutions giving thanks for the revival led to a lengthy discussion about the growth of smaller groups. The Revd Hugh Carson of Ballyweaney expressed regret 'that the report contained no allusion to the efforts of certain sectaries, who were endeavouring to sow heresies among country congregations'. Carson urged that efforts should be made to counter the errors of the Baptists and 'to check the heresy of the Plymouth Brethren, which was spreading in many parts of the country'. His claim was dismissed as an exaggeration by others. The Revd Joseph Macdonnell of Coleraine thought Carson was 'magnifying into undue importance things really almost unworthy of notice'. Dr Marcus Dill of Ballykelly, a supporter of Grattan Guinness during 1859, expressed his sorrow 'that one result of the late Revival was the propagation by Plymouth Brethren, and others of a spirit of sectarianism and division'. Yet Dill believed the Presbyterian Church had nothing to fear, since the Brethren and Baptists would not prosper, and it 'could afford to treat them, he would not say with contempt, but with indifference'. The Revd Hugh Hamilton of Cullybackey agreed, and pointed to the failure of McVicker to attract a following in Ballymena as evidence of this.

Despite the claims of Carson's colleagues, the concerns he raised were shared by many Presbyterians, who, in a flurry of publications, criticised the Brethren in general and McVicker specifically. Certainly, disquiet about the Brethren had already spread to Belfast, the provincial capital. In July 1863, the Presbyterian *Londonderry Standard* reported a public clash between Grattan Guinness and the Revd Hugh Hanna of Berry Street congregation in Belfast.[40] In a sermon preached on 5 July in the town, Guinness stated that he had 'never anywhere encountered so much religious profession worth so little of religious vitality as I have seen among the Presbyterians of Scotland and Ulster'. Hanna was outraged and announced that he would attend every public meeting Guinness addressed to challenge his calumnies and his Brethren views. The prospects of a public showdown were dealt a blow when the mayor of Belfast ruled that neither should speak in public, owing to 'the usual "Twelfth of July" riots'. The *Standard* was critical of Guinness because he had betrayed the support he had received while preaching in Derry during 1859. As a consequence, the *Standard* thought it 'exceedingly necessary that his late aberrations, both of doctrine and practice, should be made publicly known'. Since the revival, the Brethren had 'made for themselves a questionable reputation' in Derry, and because Guinness was associated with them, 'too searching a scrutiny can hardly be made both into the conduct of its agents and into the nature of the peculiar doctrines which it is their business to propagate'.

In January 1864, the *Banner of Ulster* reported that 'the Belfast affair' was being discussed extensively in the Edinburgh *Witness*. Guinness was due to visit the General Assembly of the Free Church of Scotland, and so Hanna had written a series of letters showing that Guinness was no friend of Presbyterianism, had 'adopted, with one exception, the chief peculiarities of the Plymouth Brethren', and had subverted his calling as an evangelist by becoming 'the agent of a sect'. The *Banner* noted that 'Mr. Guinness is not often treated to such sober and needful criticism, and it can hardly fail to have a salutary effect.'[41]

The problem was that Presbyterians, Baptists, Brethren and other evangelicals all welcomed the Ulster revival and endeavoured to vindicate its spiritual reality; Hanna and other Presbyterians had even supported Guinness during 1859. Yet Guinness was associated with Brethren views, and the numerical gains made after the revival by the Brethren and the Baptists were at the expense of the Presbyterian Church. The uncertainty that this caused Presbyterian critics can be seen in articles written for the *Evangelical Witness and Presbyterian Review* by the Revd John Hall of Armagh, and later of Fifth Avenue Presbyterian Church in New York. Hall's first article on the Brethren appeared in January 1863; in it, he criticised a number of their theological errors and argued that these would inevitably lead to the abandonment of any orthodox creed and the adoption of rationalism. Hall had written the article as the Brethren had been energetic in disseminating their views under a variety of labels, and in a bewildering variety of forms, and it was necessary to determine how far his Presbyterian readership could cooperate with them.[42] Hall returned to the issue in January 1865, and identified the Brethren as an example of one of two opposing forces at work in contemporary Christianity; on the one hand, the robust defence of denominational principles, and, on the other, 'a vigorous assault upon all Churches'.[43] Which side should Presbyterians take? As for the Brethren, Hall praised 'their freedom, their extempore prayer, their zeal, their activity, their directness, and their recognition of the priesthood of all God's people', yet he regretted their rejection of the New Testament model of church government and the ordained ministry.[44] Although Presbyterians dismissed the High Church understanding of apostolic succession and holy orders, they shared a commitment to church order, and so rejected what they regarded as the chaotic primitivism of the Brethren.

As the Brethren continued to grow throughout the 1860s, Presbyterian writers published pamphlets critical of their beliefs and practices. In 1864, the Revd J. B. Rentoul of Garvagh in County Londonderry issued his refutation of Brethren principles. As with every other Presbyterian writer on the subject, Rentoul began by noting that it was difficult to know what the Brethren believed, since they had no creed and were divided into a bewildering number of factions. After an examination of their beliefs in the light of the Bible, he was 'convinced that the whole system of Plymouthism is antagonistic to the unerring standard of Divine truth, subversive alike of the essential doctrines, as well as of the leading ordinances of our holy religion, and consequently most dangerous to the immortal interests of man'. No less serious was the practical outcome of Brethren teaching, 'to derange the order of the Church, and undermine the faith of Christians, without providing anything substantial in the place of her present organization'.[45] To illustrate his general conclusions, Rentoul traced throughout the rest of his publication how Brethren belief overturned orthodox understandings of the Christian Sabbath, the gospel ministry, prayer, assurance of salvation, the person and righteousness of Christ, and the moral law.

All Presbyterian critics claimed the Brethren taught that assurance of salvation was achieved instantaneously and consciously at the point of conversion. Traditional Presbyterian views on assurance were more subtle. They did not deny that infallible assurance could be achieved, though they believed most would wait long to do so, and they avoided a general application of infallible assurance to all believers because it might promote self-righteousness and antinomianism.[46] Yet instantaneous and infallible assurance had been popularised during the 1859 revival, and in the mid-1860s the Presbyterian Church experienced the so-called Assurance Controversy, which concluded with a fudge that implicitly accepted the novel views.[47] For critics such as the Revd William Dobbin, this amounted to the adoption of Plymouth Brethren doctrine.[48] The Assurance Controversy showed the potential effect of the Brethren on Presbyterian belief, and it was the fifth-column character of the movement that concerned Presbyterians. The minister of Seskinore in County Tyrone, the Revd John Smyth, did not mince his words: 'Plymouthism – concealing the stiletto of the Spiritual assassin beneath the folds of a professed charity, and enclosing its errors in the enamelled case of an exuberant zeal – is a mirage in the desert of Spiritual destitution, that draws men but to deceive them.' In the final analysis, it was 'a most insidious, constructive conspiracy against the Churches of Christendom'.[49]

The Brethren threat was notable in Ulster, but it was evident also in the other three Irish provinces where Catholics comprised almost 90 per cent of the population and unity among the protestant minority was therefore imperative. In an article published in the *Evangelical Witness* in 1865, the Revd W. B. Kirkpatrick, a Presbyterian minister in Dublin, noted that the greatest threat to the Church of Ireland, by far the largest protestant church in the south, was 'the movements of the lay-preachers and of the Plymouth Brethren'. The influence of these was especially injurious, 'because it operates from within the Church itself, and is detaching from it some of those who appeared to be most able and willing to give to it increased efficiency in the land'.[50] Certainly, members of the Irish state church were alert to the danger. The *London Quarterly Review* in October 1866 published a lengthy review of pamphlets written against the Brethren and lay preachers by Church of Ireland writers, including Edward A. Stopford, archdeacon of Meath, William R. Bailey, rector of Monaghan, and Edward Nangle, premillennialist, founder of the Achill Mission to Roman Catholics, and rector of Skreen, County Sligo. The reviewer illustrated the threat posed by the Brethren, drawing attention to 'the number, devotedness, and wealth of its adherents', and to their distribution of thousands of tracts.[51] The review concluded that Plymouthism was 'a perilous and mischievous heresy' that had undermined efforts at spreading the gospel throughout the United Kingdom. To combat the threat, all clergymen must guard against its influence. In particular, the state churches in England and Ireland ought to employ 'lay preachers and prayer leaders' as its formal structures 'repelled' the laity interested in these roles and led individuals to 'overleap all bounds and barriers, and become roving evangelists without a church, a commission, or a creed'.[52] Such was the perceived influence of the Brethren within the Church of Ireland that commentators saw its baleful effect on efforts to pare back the Irish Prayer Book after disestablishment in 1870. The *Irish Ecclesiastical Gazette* acknowledged Brethren influence on that issue, concluding that 'they have done much mischief by breaking into folds, violating the unity, of Christ's Church, disturbing humble Christians, and separating choice friends'.[53] Concerns about Brethren gains at the expense of the Church of Ireland would be repeated during the visits to southern Ireland of D. L. Moody and Ira D. Sankey in 1874 and 1883.[54]

The southern Irish experience was likely formative for the most widely published Presbyterian critic of the Brethren, the Revd Thomas Croskery.[55] A convert to Presbyterian evangelicalism from Unitarianism, Croskery probably had direct experience of Exclusive Brethren lay preachers whilst the minister of Clonakilty, County Cork, between 1863 and 1866. He subsequently became minister of Waterside congregation in Derry, before his appointment in 1875 as a professor of theology at Magee College in the city. Croskery's first publication on the Brethren was an essay in the *Eclectic Review*, published in September 1864, and entitled, 'Darbyism and Lay-Preaching in Ireland'. This offered a balanced-yet-critical assessment of a movement that in the south was dominated by young, well-off men who were fashionably dressed and often wore 'beard and moustache'.[56] In assessing their impact, Croskery noted that they had made genuine converts, offered a stimulus to ministry in the Church of Ireland, especially amongst the laity, and promoted Bible study in general, yet the evangelical churches would not reap the benefit. Although primarily about southern Ireland, the *Coleraine Chronicle* reproduced lengthy extracts 'from Mr Croskery's article in the *Eclectic*'. They noted the relevance of his analysis to Ulster and called for the article to be published as a tract, for it was 'altogether an admirable exposure of the errors and fallacies of Plymouth Brethrenism'.[57]

Croskery's geographical frame of reference was extensive, and he drew parallels between the effect of the Brethren on protestant minorities in the south of Ireland, Italy and France. In an article published in the *British and Foreign Evangelical Review* in July 1865, he interpreted the Brethren as contributing to the age-old heresy of antinomianism, which denied the perpetual obligation of Christian believers to obey the moral law. This heresy was 'the pest of revived Christianity ever since the days of the apostles', and in some respects, it was as dangerous as 'philosophic rationalism and intellectual infidelity'.[58] On the basis of personal experience in Ireland, and knowledge of developments in continental Europe, it was clear that the aim of the Brethren was 'gathering churches out of churches'.[59] They began in neighbourhoods by declaring their catholicity, but quickly produced 'the most rampant sectarianism, aggravated in many instances by the bitterness which attends apostasy from evangelical communions'. At the same time, 'their Antinomian tendencies' led to 'indiscriminate fault-finding' and 'an inordinate spiritual conceit' that produced self-righteousness and spiritual pride.[60] Croskery returned to the moral effects of the Brethren in an article published in 1869. Again, he began with the general observation that religious revival produced a tendency to overturn accepted forms, and commented on the fissiparous and strife-ridden character of Brethren assemblies. Yet as the movement, especially in the Exclusive variety, had no means of propagating itself, Croskery concluded that separatism, 'is really nothing more than a rash on the surface of the body ecclesiastic, which is hot and fiery for a time, and then disappears in an incredibly short space of time'.[61]

Croskery did not confine his criticisms to weighty articles in journals. In the summer of 1865, the first edition of his *A Catechism on the Doctrines of the Plymouth Brethren* was published in London by James Nisbet, and fourth and fifth expanded editions appeared the following year.[62] The catechism was positively reviewed, and would remain in print on both sides of the Atlantic for the next two decades. Croskery was aware of significant differences of opinion among the Brethren, but believed that their influence was such that four-fifths of lay preachers in Ireland were tainted by their erroneous doctrine. They grew by poaching church members, 'a new style of Christianity that prompts its disciples to conceal their opinions, and admits of all kinds of dexterous evasions to accomplish their divisive and sectarian objects. It is a style that is neither Christ-like nor apostolic'.[63] The sixth edition of the catechism, published in 1868, was much expanded, contained rewritten sections on the ministry and the church, and included two new chapters on baptism.

Criticism, Moody and Sankey and Politics, 1870–1912

Croskery's catechism was reprinted many times because the Brethren continued to make headlines. In March 1870, for instance, it was reported that two Brethren lay preachers, self-described as a 'converted thief from London' and 'a fool for Christ's sake from Belfast', had been attracting large crowds in Lurgan, County Armagh. They announced their intention to perform baptism in nearby Lough Neagh, the largest freshwater lake in Britain and Ireland. On Sunday afternoon, a crowd of between four and five hundred congregated at the lough's edge, 'regardless of the dirt and water through which they ran'; a factory girl was reported to have remarked that she 'never thought the river Jordan was so near before'.[64] In the light of such incidents, presbytery reports submitted to the General Assembly in June 1871 noted that the 'Plymouth Brethren are making efforts, not in teaching the ignorant, but in seeking to proselytise the thoughtful', a point underlined in a pamphlet by the Revd David Hunter of Mountpottinger, Belfast.[65] The challenge in the early 1870s of Brethren theology to confessional Presbyterianism concerned Robert Watts, the denomination's professor of theology and the foremost proponent of 'Princeton Theology' in the United Kingdom.[66] In a series of lectures delivered throughout Presbyterian Ulster, Watts refuted the errors of 'Plymouth Brethrenism' with special reference to their dispensationalism.[67] This had only been an incidental aspect of Presbyterian critiques, and Watts's dismissal of the personal reign of Christ and a premillennial advent was a product of his own postmillennialism.

Once again, the revival heartland of mid Antrim produced anti-Brethren publications throughout the 1870s.[68] The Revd David Adams of Broughshane spoke for all critics when he lambasted the threat that the Brethren posed to the unity of the Church universal: 'they are little people that live in a nutshell, which they mistake for the universe, that have their own little Bethel, or "church in the house", and their own little Hymn-book, and their own little sectarian movements, and their own little heaven'. In particular, the followers of Darby were 'a very noisy sect of them', although all varieties were the 'enemies of the church of God within her own bosom'.[69] Likewise, the Revd S. J. Moore in *The Plymouth Plunge and Puzzle* described the Brethren as a 'missionary church' whose mission was 'not to the world to save the perishing, but to the Churches to pervert unsettled members'.[70] In April 1871, Moore's tract was reviewed under the title 'Religious Warfare' in both the *Ballymoney Free Press* and the *Coleraine Chronicle*, along with the Revd William Macloy's *Stones of the Temple*. The reviewer described Macloy's pamphlet as 'admirable', 'lucid' and 'highly useful' in its description of the orthodox Presbyterian position on salvation by grace in response to the Brethren position that faith led instantaneously to salvation and assurance.[71] As if to confirm the prejudices of Presbyterian critics, McVicker, self-described as 'Servant of Jesus Christ, Ballymena', responded to Macloy and Moore by reiterating his claim that 'the great mass' of the population of Ulster were 'religious without being born again. I know that telling them this gives offence, but I cannot help it.'[72]

Matters did not improve with the arrival in Ireland of the American evangelists Dwight L. Moody and Ira D. Sankey in September 1874.[73] The religious revival that they unleashed re-energised evangelicals in Ulster, but, once more, concerns were raised about lay preachers who sought to capitalise on Moody's success. Even before their arrival, some Presbyterians were uneasy about the American evangelists. In April, the Synod of Derry and Omagh heard reports from those who had witnessed Moody and Sankey's success in Scotland. They were hopeful that a revival could be promoted that avoided the excesses and errors of 1859, yet there was concern that it would not be the Presbyterian Church but the Brethren who would gain adherents. For instance, the Revd N. M. Brown of Limavady stressed that 'much of these revivals ended in Antinomianism and in the detaching of some of their best people from the Presbyterian Church'.[74] The Revd Thomas Houston, a Reformed Presbyterian minister, declaimed the 'serious and fundamental' errors of the Brethren. These errors were propagated by 'certain classes of Revivalist preachers' whose techniques were, in turn, employed by Moody. Given that doctrines 'not accordant with the system of grace revealed in the Bible' were being taught, Houston was critical of the support given by Presbyterian ministers to Moody.[75]

Houston expressed a widespread concern that lay preachers inspired by Moody were undermining genuine faith as well as highlighting Moody's own warm relationship with the Open Brethren.[76] In December 1875, the Presbytery of Belfast passed a resolution against employing evangelists 'who are not in the membership of any evangelical denomination, and whose soundness in the faith we have not sufficient evidence'. A protest was submitted at the meeting of the Belfast Synod in April 1876 and signed by supporters of Moody, including Robert Watts.[77] Aside from the specific issue of lay evangelists, there was a renewed effort to reinforce correct doctrine among ordinary Presbyterians. At the Presbytery meeting in December, ministers were exhorted 'to meet the prevailing errors of the present time and guard the faith and morals of those committed to our care'. They ought to do so by instructing their congregations on 'those points of doctrine and discipline which are being specially assailed, and to use their best endeavours that our people shall be carefully instructed in the standards of the Presbyterian Church'.[78] The nearby Presbytery of Comber arranged for the delivery of sermons in all their congregations on subjects that aimed to refute the errors of lay preachers and the Brethren.[79] Part of the reason was due to the actions of an elder in Killyleagh congregation, Captain Joseph Gilmore, who was charged with promoting the Plymouth Brethren in violation of his ordination vows to uphold Presbyterian church order.[80]

The continued threat of the Brethren prompted Croskery to publish a book-length refutation in 1879. Croskery acknowledged that many godly individuals were associated with the Brethren in the early days, and offered positive comments on A. N. Groves, Samuel Prideaux Tregelles, Henry Craik, and, especially, B. W. Newton. The main problem was Darby, who single-handedly caused the Plymouth schism of 1848. Croskery restated his argument that the errors of the Brethren, especially in its Darbyite form, were simply a rehash of age-old heresies and those associated with a diverse range of modern writers such as Edward Irving and John Henry Newman. He also criticised the Brethren attitude to separation from the 'doomed world', which entailed opposition to missionary and religious societies and a repudiation of the efforts of Christians to end slavery and infanticide, reform prisons and establish hospitals.[81] Croskery ascribed the success of the Brethren to the yearning for greater spirituality in the 1820s, the novelty of their views on eschatology, and the boldness of their leaders. Ultimately, the Brethren, especially the Exclusives, 'live upon the industry of their neighbours – finding it more convenient to plunder the Church than to gather in the outcasts from the lanes and byways'.[82] To hasten its downfall, churches must maintain their soundness and piety and engage in spreading the true gospel. Despite growing evangelical unity, the Brethren could yet split the Church, and Croskery ended his analysis with a warning that 'it ought to be the prayer of all the churches that the Lord would guard His people against the seductions of a system which, if it obtained general currency, would reproduce in these latter days those disastrous strifes and wanderings which divided the primitive ages of the Church'.[83] Croskery modified his prognosis somewhat in an obituary notice of Darby, who died on 29 April 1882. There, he talked about the numerical failure of the Brethren and ascribed this to the revived state of the mainstream protestant churches and evangelical unity in missionary activism.[84]

As the nineteenth century drew to a close, the Brethren continued to be viewed with suspicion. A new criticism was their lack of involvement in politics, especially as the threat of Home Rule for Ireland united northern Protestants against the possibility of a Catholic-dominated 'Rome Rule' parliament in Dublin.[85] This article has already noted the link made by critics between the Brethren and Roman

Catholicism; for instance, J. C. L. Carson described the 'Jesuitical' character of the movement, and Croskery discerned an affinity with the ideas of the future Cardinal John Henry Newman. More prosaically, Brethren numbers were sizeable enough to make a difference in marginal constituencies in Ulster where it was imperative to maximise the protestant pro-Union vote. The problem was that voting in elections was discouraged among the Brethren, owing to their separatism.[86] The editor of the *Northern Whig* noted this during the nomination process for the East Tyrone constituency in July 1886. The prospective Unionist candidate, M. G. Megaw, had 'a tough battle' in this majority Catholic district, but there was a good chance of success if 'all the Loyalists' joined together. In the previous election, both the Brethren and Reformed Presbyterians did not vote, and although the *Whig* respected their conscientious convictions, the duty of voting could not be set aside, 'for the issues at stake are vital, and abstention means the strengthening of the enemy'. An inspection of the nomination papers showed that some members of these groups had supported Megaw, and the *Whig* hoped their example would be followed because 'every single Loyalist vote is wanted'.[87] Megaw lost the election by 468 votes.[88] A similar situation arose in the Derry City by-election in February 1899, when the Unionist candidate failed to oust the sitting Nationalist MP by forty-two votes.[89] An angry letter appeared in the *Belfast Telegraph* from Frederick Christie, assistant secretary of the Protestant Association, who blamed the defeat on Brethren and Reformed Presbyterians who did not vote. For the same reason, Christie claimed that seats had been lost in East Donegal, Derry City, North Tyrone, and South Down. The solution was clear: both groups had to do their duty and unite with their fellow protestants.[90] Despite such calls, the majority of the Brethren remained unmoved, and their attitude is best captured in their response to one of the major set pieces of Ulster Unionist opposition to Home Rule. On 28 September 1912, 77% of the eligible protestant male population signed the Ulster Covenant that pledged to use all means necessary 'to defeat the present conspiracy to set up a Home Rule Parliament in Ireland'.[91] By contrast, the rate among evangelical 'others' was 38.7%; among that cohort, the Brethren had the lowest rate of 31.4%.[92]

Criticism of the Brethren by Presbyterians continued into the late nineteenth century, although it became less frequent. The presence of the Brethren in County Tyrone prompted the publication of the last stand-alone Presbyterian critique by the Revd William T. Latimer of Eglish, who in 1883, delivered and published a lecture to his congregation about the dangers of Brethren belief and practice.[93] By 1908, Latimer's *Lecture on the Doctrines of Plymouth Brethren* had reached its seventh edition and 16,000 copies. He was sure that the Open Brethren were as bad as the Darbyites, and together Plymouthism began as 'the most liberal, and it ends with being the most exclusive system in the world'.[94] The lecture included criticism of the Cooneyites, another primitivist group that originated in County Fermanagh and was often lumped together with the Brethren.[95] It was the self-righteousness and exclusivity of both groups that exercised Latimer. Referring to the Cooneyites, he noted that 'they condemn everybody, who does not belong to their sect, and some of their more ignorant members state that until they began to preach the whole world was going right to eternal destruction'.[96] Latimer's lecture reflected his unease about the 1859 revival. In *A History of the Irish Presbyterians* (1902), he noted with regret the growth of Methodists, Baptists, Independents and Salvation Army after the revival, although the Brethren were 'the most fanatical and exclusive'.[97] Latimer also noted the growing threat of freelance evangelists and non-sectarian associations employing male and female lay-preachers. Undoubtedly, individuals were converted at these missions and some joined local congregations, but others got too high an opinion of themselves and ended up in the Brethren. Latimer believed that the Presbyterian Church had 'failed to grapple with the new conditions arising from' the revival, and that it was imperative for the denomination to harness this lay enthusiasm for the good of the church.[98]

Conclusions

The growth of the Brethren and the popularity of lay preachers after 1859 was especially problematic for Presbyterians. Both were reminders of the unwelcome aspects of the revival, and threatened Presbyterian ownership of what was considered the spiritual high point of Ulster Protestantism in the last two hundred years. For the protestant minority throughout Ireland, the growth of the Brethren and other smaller denominations also threatened protestant unity against the increasing threat of a Home Rule parliament in Dublin, dominated by Catholics who were said to be controlled by Rome through their priests. Presbyterians responded to these threats by publishing a large number of works critical of the Brethren, but the denomination also incorporated aspects of popular religious practice in an effort to harness the religious energy displayed. As a consequence, the primitivism represented by the Brethren, albeit in an exaggerated form, strengthened a more general evangelical religious culture and contributed to the dilution of denominational identity. The implications of this were evident in 1927 when Professor J. E. Davey of the Presbyterian Church in Ireland was accused of theological 'modernism' and subjected to a heresy trial. Davey was acquitted by a very large majority, and a significant part of his defence included an appeal to the type of personal religious experience that had been popularised during the 1859 revival. This appeal made it very difficult for his accusers, who had the sympathy of the Brethren, to portray Davey as a heretic because they were equally a product of that 'year of grace'.[99] In that regard, Presbyterian critics were correct that the Brethren brand of evangelical populism undermined denominational principles and practice.

As suggested by Coad and Grass, the legacy of Presbyterian criticism was also important in shaping the rigid outlook of the Brethren in Northern Ireland, who had, by 1951, reached a high point of 17,845 self-described adherents.[100] Yet despite their separatism and modest numbers, the Brethren had a marked effect on the popular religious culture of protestants in the north of Ireland. The primitivist impulse represented and encouraged by their Gospel Halls was apparent in a populist evangelical religiosity associated with autonomous mission halls in rural and urban areas.[101] This was a fluid religious culture that sat loose with denominational structures and brought together those concerned about the salvation of souls, the cultivation of personal holiness and a sometimes-apocalyptic interpretation of contemporary events. It was from this populist evangelical subculture that Ian Paisley emerged in the late 1940s as a scourge of 'liberal' theology and ecumenism, critic of the Unionist establishment and anti-Catholic firebrand.[102] In religious terms, the Brethren had much in common with Paisley, yet they did not follow his route into populist political unionism. As the political scientist Neil Southern points out, the Brethren throughout the Troubles in Northern Ireland after 1968 remained largely apolitical, and this underlines the point that theological conservatism does not necessarily produce strident politics.[103] The evangelical populism represented by the Brethren is a reminder that religious faith, even in the north of Ireland, has a dynamism of its own that cannot simply be reduced to political identity and division.

Notes

The author acknowledges with gratitude that the research for this article was funded by a Research Project Grant from the Leverhulme Trust. He would like to thank for their comments on earlier versions: Crawford Gribben, David N. Livingstone, Stuart Mathieson, and the two anonymous readers.

1. M. A. Noll, 'National Churches, Gathered Churches, and Varieties of Lay Evangelicalism, 1735–1859', in D. W. Lovegrove (ed.), *The Rise of the Laity in Evangelical Protestantism* (London: Routledge, 2002), pp. 134–52.
2. N. O. Hatch, *The Democratization of American Christianity* (New Haven/London: Yale University Press, 1989).
3. D. H. Akenson, *The Americanization of the Apocalypse: Creating America's Own Bible* (New York: Oxford University Press, 2023), p. 20.
4. D. H. Akenson, *Discovering the End of Time: Irish Evangelicals in the Age of Daniel O'Connell* (Montreal and Kingston/London: McGill-Queen's University Press, 2015); *Exporting the Rapture: John Nelson Darby and the Victorian Conquest of North-American Evangelicalism* (New York: Oxford University Press, 2018); Akenson, *Americanization*.
5. D. W. Bebbington, 'The Place of the Brethren Movement in International Evangelicalism', in N. T. R. Dickson and Tim Grass (eds), *The Growth of the Brethren Movement: National and International Experiences: Essays in Honour of Harold H. Rawdon* (Milton Keynes: Paternoster, 2006), p. 260.
6. F. R. Coad, *A History of the Brethren movement: Its Origins, its Worldwide Development and its Significance for the Present Day* (Exeter: Paternoster Press, 1976), p. 231.
7. Tim Grass, *Gathering to His Name: The Story of Open Brethren in Britain and Ireland* (Milton Keynes: Paternoster, 2006), pp. 217–26.
8. Grass, *Gathering*, p. 214.

9   *Ibid.*, p. 126; Coad, *History of the Brethren*, p. 172.
10 The most up-to-date and suggestive study is Crawford Gribben, *J. N. Darby and the Roots of Dispensationalism* (New York: Oxford University Press, 2024).
11 The growth of the Brethren in Ulster after 1859 has been noted by, for instance, Coad, *History*, pp. 169–72; David Hempton and Myrtle Hill, *Evangelical Protestantism in Ulster Society 1740–1890* (London: Routledge, 1992), p. 155; Janice Holmes, 'Transformation, aberration or Consolidation? Explaining the Ulster Revival of 1859', in Niall Ó Ciosáin (ed.), *Explaining Change in Cultural History* (Dublin: University College Dublin Press, 2005), pp. 126–7.
12 Grass, *Gathering*, p. 217.
13 I am indebted to S. J. Brown for the following discussion of the condition of the Church of Ireland: Brown, *The National Churches of England, Ireland, and Scotland, 1801–1846* (Oxford: Oxford University Press, 2001).
14 Grayson Carter, *Anglican Evangelicals: Protestant Secessions from the Via Media, c.1800–1850* (Oxford: Oxford University Press, 2001), pp. 152–248.
15 Akenson, *Discovering the End of Time*.
16 I. S. Rennie, 'Aspects of Christian Brethren Spirituality', in J. I. Packer and Loren Wilkinson (eds), *Alive to God: Studies in Spirituality, Presented to James Houston* (Downers Grove, IL: InterVarsity Press, 1992), p. 190.
17 Grass, *Gathering*, pp. 115–46.
18 N. T. R. Dickson, '"The Church Itself is God's Clergy": The Principles and Practices of the Brethren', in Lovegrove (ed.), *Rise of the Laity*, p. 222.
19 *Ibid.*, p. 227.
20 For a recent overview of the revival and how it has been interpreted, see A. R. Holmes, 'The Ulster Revival of 1859: Causes, Controversies and Consequences', *Journal of Ecclesiastical History*, 63 (2012), 488–515.
21 William Gibson, *The Year of Grace: A History of the Revival in Ireland, A.D. 1859 ... With an Introduction by Rev. Baron Stow, D.D.* (Boston: Gould and Lincoln, 1860).
22 Daniel Ritchie, 'The 1859 Revival and its Enemies: Opposition to Religious Revivalism Within Ulster Presbyterianism', *Irish Historical Studies*, 40 (2016), 66–91; Daniel Ritchie, *Isaac Nelson: Radical Abolitionist, Evangelical Presbyterian, and Irish Nationalist* (Liverpool: Liverpool University Press, 2018), pp. 125–84.
23 'Report on the State of Religion', *Missionary Herald of the Presbyterian Church in Ireland* (September 1859), p. 402.
24 A. R. Holmes, *The Irish Presbyterian Mind: Conservative Theology, Evangelical Experience, and Modern Criticism, 1830–1930* (Oxford: Oxford University Press, 2018), pp. 51–3, 66–9.
25 Henry Grattan Guinness, *The Revival in Ireland. Letters From Ministers and Medical Men in Ulster on the Revival of Religion in the North of Ireland* (Philadelphia: William S. and Alfred Martien, 1860).
26 'The Awakening in Ulster. Part III', *Things New and Old*, 2 (1859), p. 184.
27 *Ibid.*, p. 185.

28 William Crook, *Lay-preaching in Ireland, and the New Gospel. A Tract for the Times* (London: Hamilton, Adams, and Co., 1865), p. 12.
29 Coad, *History*, pp. 228, 229.
30 *Coleraine Chronicle* (8 March 1862), p. 4.
31 J. C. L. Carson, *The Heresies of the Plymouth Brethren* (London: Houlston and Sons, 1883), p. v.
32 *Ibid.*, p. vi.
33 Joshua Thompson, 'Irish Baptists and the 1859 Revival', *Irish Baptist Historical Society Journal*, 17 (1984–85), 9. More generally, see R. C. McMullan, 'Irish Baptist Attitudes to the First Century of Brethrenism', *Irish Baptist Historical Society Journal*, new series 4 (1996–97), 7–23.
34 For McVicker, see Crawford Gribben, '"The Worst Sect that a Christian Man Can Meet": Opposition to the Plymouth Brethren in Ireland and Scotland, 1859–1900', *Scottish Studies Review*, 3 (2002), 34–6.
35 'The Baptist Church', *Ballymena Observer* (13 December 1862), p. 1.
36 'The "Plymouth Brethren"', *Ballymena Observer* (20 December 1862), p. 1.
37 All figures taken from *Census of Ireland, 1911. Area, Houses, and Population: Also the Ages, Civil or Conjugal Condition, Occupations, Birthplaces, Religion, and Education of the People. Province of Ulster. Summary Tables* (Dublin: His Majesty's Stationery Office, 1912), p. 38.
38 Nicola Morris, 'Predicting a "Bright and Prosperous Future": Irish Methodist Membership (1855–1915)', *Wesley and Methodist Studies*, 2 (2010), 91–114; A. R. Holmes and Stuart Mathieson, 'Evangelical "Others" in Ulster, 1859–1912: Social Profile, Unionist Politics, and "Fundamentalism"', *Church History*, 90 (2021), 847–72.
39 'Synod of Ballymena and Coleraine', *Coleraine Chronicle* (25 May 1861), p. 3. All quotations in this paragraph are taken from this source.
40 'Sectarian attacks on Presbyterianism', *Londonderry Standard* (18 July 1863), p. 2. All quotations in this paragraph are taken from this source.
41 'Rev. H. G. Guinness in Edinburgh', *Banner of Ulster* (14 January 1864), p. 3.
42 John Hall, 'The "Christian Brethren"', *Evangelical Witness and Presbyterian Review*, 2 (January 1863), 11–14.
43 John Hall, 'Where We Stand', *Evangelical Witness and Presbyterian Review*, 4 (January 1865), p. 20.
44 *Ibid.*, p. 21.
45 J. B. Rentoul, *A Refutation of the Leading Principles of the Plymouth Brethren* (Belfast: C. Aitchison, 1864), p. iii.
46 A. R. Holmes, 'Personal Conversion, Revival, and the Holy Spirit: Presbyterian Evangelicalism in Early Nineteenth-Century Ulster', in John Coffey (ed.), *Heart Religion: Evangelical Piety in England and Ireland, 1690–1850* (Oxford: Oxford University Press, 2016), pp. 181–200.
47 Daniel Ritchie, 'Confessional Calvinism and Evangelical Assurance: Isaac Nelson, Ulster Revivalism, and the Assurance Controversy in the Presbyterian Church in Ireland, c.1859–1867', *History*, 100 (2015), 85–106.

48 'Special Meeting of the Banbridge Presbytery', *Londonderry Standard* (17 June 1865), p. 1; *Belfast Morning News* (13 June 1866), p. 3.

49 John Smyth, *Plymouth Brethrenism: Its Creed and Character. A Dialogue* (Glasgow: W. Love, [1869]), p. 2.

50 W. B. Kirkpatrick, 'The Presbyterian Church in the South of Ireland', *Evangelical Witness and Presbyterian Review*, 4 (October 1865), p. 270.

51 'The Plymouth Brethren and Lay Preaching in Ireland', *London Quarterly Review*, 27 (October 1866), p. 8.

52 *Ibid.*, p. 37.

53 'The Plymouth Brethren', *Irish Ecclesiastical Gazette* (22 October 1870), p. 263.

54 A. R. Holmes and Stuart Mathieson, 'Dwight L. Moody in Southern Ireland: Modern Evangelical Revivalism, the Protestant Minority, and the Conversion of Catholic Ireland', *Journal of Religious History*, 47 (2023), 287–8.

55 William Irwin, 'Our Own Worthies. The Rev. Thomas Croskery, D.D.', *Presbyterian Churchman* (1886), pp. 313–20.

56 [Thomas Croskery], 'Darbyism and Lay-Preaching in Ireland', *Eclectic Review*, 7 (September 1864), p. 317.

57 'Literature', *Coleraine Chronicle* (17 September 1864), p. 6.

58 Thomas Croskery, 'Plymouthism and Dr Whately', *British and Foreign Evangelical Review*, 14 (1865), p. 470.

59 *Ibid.*, p. 486.

60 *Ibid.*, p. 487.

61 Thomas Croskery, 'The Separatist Theory of a Pure Church', *British and Foreign Evangelical Review*, 18 (1869), p. 75.

62 Details from Thomas Croskery, *A Catechism of the Doctrine of the Plymouth Brethren*, 6th edition (London: James Nisbet and Co., 1868).

63 *Ibid.*, p. 2.

64 'Baptism by Immersion in Lough Neagh', *Newry Reporter* (26 March 1870), p. 3.

65 'Annual Report on the State of Religion', *Missionary Herald of the Presbyterian Church in Ireland* (July and August 1871), p. 375. David Hunter, *Plymouthists and Their Principles* (Belfast: Bible and Colportage Society of Ireland, n.d.).

66 Holmes, *Irish Presbyterian Mind*, pp. 57–9.

67 'Millenarianism', *Belfast News-Letter* (27 March 1871), p. 3; 'Newry Presbyterian Young Men's Society', *Newry Commercial Telegraph* (2 November 1871), p. 3; *Coleraine Chronicle* (17 February 1872), p. 4.

68 For a later example, David McMeekin, *Plymouthists: Their Doctrines and Their Doings* (Ballymena: M. Erwin, [1876]).

69 David Adams, *Lecture on Presbyterianism as Contrasted with Plymouthism. Delivered on 6th March, 1870, in First Presbyterian Church Broughshane* (Ballymena: William Erwin, 1870), p. 6.

70 S. J. Moore, *The Plymouth Plunge and Puzzle* (Ballymena: William Erwin, 1871), p. 5.

71 'Religious Warfare', *Coleraine Chronicle* (15 April 1871), p. 3.

72 J. G. McVicker, *Salvation by Faith: Set Forth and Vindicated ... Second edition, with Appendix and Notes* (Ballymena: William Erwin and John Kee, 1871), p. 16.

73 A. R. Holmes and Stuart Mathieson, 'Dwight L. Moody in Ulster: Evangelical Unity, Denominational Identity, and the Fundamentalist Impulse', *Journal of Ecclesiastical History*, 72 (2021), 800–21.
74 'The Religious Awakening in Scotland', *Londonderry Sentinel* (30 April 1874), p. 2.
75 Thomas Houston, *Plymouthism and Revivalism: Part Second, on Regeneration, Justification, and Sanctification, Scripturally Stated, in Opposition to Plymouthist and Revivalist Errors* (Belfast: C. Aitchison, [1874]), p. 43.
76 Akenson, *Americanization*, pp. 225-52.
77 'The Presbyterian Church. Presbytery of Belfast', *Northern Whig* (7 December 1875), p. 8; 'Synod of Belfast', *Belfast News-Letter* (20 April 1876), p. 4.
78 'The Presbyterian Church. Presbytery of Belfast'.
79 'The Presbyterian Church. Presbytery of Comber', *Belfast News-Letter* (16 May 1876), p. 4.
80 'The Plymouth Brethren – The Presbytery of Comber', *Northern Whig* (30 March 1876), p. 5.
81 Thomas Croskery, *Plymouth-Brethrenism: A Refutation of its Principles and Doctrines* (Belfast: William Mullan and Son, 1879), p. 151.
82 *Ibid.*, p. 165.
83 *Ibid.*, p. 168.
84 Thomas Croskery, 'John Nelson Darby', *Catholic Presbyterian*, 7 (June 1882), 440–5.
85 Hempton and Hill, *Evangelical Protestantism*, pp. 161–87.
86 N. T. R. Dickson, *Brethren in Scotland, 1838-2000: A Social Study of an Evangelical Movement* (Carlisle: Paternoster, 2003), p. 310.
87 *Northern Whig* (8 July 1886), p. 4.
88 B. M. Walker (ed.), *Parliamentary Election Results in Ireland, 1801-1922* (Dublin: Royal Irish Academy, 1978), p. 377.
89 *Ibid.*, p. 362.
90 'How Derry Was Lost', *Belfast Telegraph* (28 February 1899), p. 4.
91 David Fitzpatrick, *Descendancy: Irish Protestant Histories Since 1795* (Cambridge: Cambridge University Press, 2014), p. 108; Patrick Buckland (ed.), *Irish Unionism 1885-1923: A Documentary History* (Belfast: Her Majesty's Stationery Office, 1973), p. 224.
92 Holmes and Mathieson, 'Evangelical "others" in Ulster', 868, 869.
93 The 1883 publication date is noted in the *Tyrone Constitution* (29 June 1894), p. 4.
94 W. T. Latimer, *A Lecture on the Doctrines of Plymouth Brethren*, 7th edition (Belfast: James Cleeland, 1908), p. 3.
95 Irvine Gray, *'Two by two': The Shape of a Shapeless Movement. A Study of a Religious Movement Started in Ireland in 1897 by William Irvine and Edward Cooney* (Portadown: Irvine Gray, 2013).
96 Latimer, *Lecture*, p. 13.
97 W. T. Latimer, *A History of the Irish Presbyterians*, 2nd edition (Belfast: James Cleeland, 1902), p. 495.
98 *Ibid.*, p. 497.

99 Holmes, *Irish Presbyterian Mind*, pp. 188–234; for Brethren support, p. 224.
100 *Census of Population of Northern Ireland 1951. General Report* (Belfast: Her Majesty's Stationery Office, 1955), p. 23.
101 Victor Maxwell, *Belfast's Halls of Faith and Fame* (Belfast: Ambassador, 1999); Judith Cole, *History of Mission Halls throughout Northern Ireland* (Belfast: Ambassador International, 2017).
102 Steve Bruce, *Paisley: Religion and Politics in Northern Ireland* (Oxford: Oxford University Press, 2007).
103 Neil Southern, 'Strong Religion and Political Viewpoints in a Deeply Divided Society: An Examination of the Gospel Hall Tradition in Northern Ireland', *Journal of Contemporary Religion*, 26 (2011), 433–49.

'Rex Dei Gratia': Mark Hovell's Forgotten Essay on *The Divine Right of Kings*

CHRIS GODDEN, UNIVERSITY OF MANCHESTER

Abstract

This article comments on a recently discovered essay, entitled 'Rex Dei Gratia', written by the Manchester historian Mark Hovell and published in the Workers' Educational Association's journal *The Highway* in the summer of 1915. Hovell's essay provides a summary of key parts of the history of the Divine Right of Kings. In addition to adding to Hovell's very limited body of historical work (it is now the only identified extant piece published during his lifetime), this discovery provides an opportunity to speculate on how Hovell might have fitted the historical theme of Divine Rights into political discourse during the First World War.

Keywords: Mark Hovell; Divine Right of Kings; *The Highway*; Workers' Educational Association; First World War

Mark Hovell was born in Manchester on 21 March 1888, one of seven children to William and Hannah Hovell, and at the age of 10, he won a scholarship at Manchester Grammar School.[1] Awarded the Hulme Scholarship at the Victoria University of Manchester to study history, he successfully graduated with a first-class honours degree in 1909.[2] Following the completion of his MA, Hovell was appointed assistant lecturer in history at the University in 1910,[3] and conducted tutorial classes in several Lancashire towns through the University's extra-mural programme, as well as teaching for the Workers' Educational Association.[4] He later secured the University's Langton Fellowship (for a period of three years), and spent the academic year 1912–13 as an assistant lecturer in English history at the Institut für Kultur- und Universalgeschichte (Institute for Cultural and Universal History) in Leipzig. He was appointed assistant lecturer in military history at the University of Manchester in October 1914. With the outbreak of the First World War, he obtained a commission in the Sherwood Foresters and was sent to the Western Front in the summer of 1916. Hovell died on 12 August 1916, and is buried in the Vermelles British Cemetery, Northern France. Obituaries recorded his death as a tragedy for his family, while also commenting on a promising academic career cut dramatically short.[5]

Hovell's reputation today rests exclusively on the posthumous publication of his book, *The Chartist Movement*. Left unfinished at the time of his death, the draft manuscript was completed by Hovell's tutor and friend, the medieval historian Thomas Tout, and published by the University of Manchester Press in early 1918.[6] Tout's efforts in completing the manuscript served as a fitting memorial to Hovell's short life, and the admirable biographical essay Tout included as an introduction to *The Chartist Movement* remains the most significant source of information on Hovell's life.[7] Aside from the biographical essay prepared by Tout, nothing of significance had been written on Hovell's life or work until a special issue of the *Bulletin of the John Rylands Library* was published in 2018.[8] This issue of the *Bulletin* was based on papers presented at a symposium to mark the centenary of Hovell's death, held as part of the Manchester Histories Festival in 2016.

Regarding the material that Hovell published during his lifetime, there is brief mention in Tout's biographical essay of a review of Felix Liebermann's *National Assembly in the Anglo-Saxon Period* (probably completed around 1913, while Hovell was staying in Leipzig) intended for publication in a French journal.[9] Despite searches in likely French historical journals, this review has yet to be identified. The posthumously completed book on Chartism therefore stood for over a century as Hovell's only identified published work, and it appeared highly unlikely that any new material, published or unpublished, would be discovered. It was therefore with great surprise – and delight – that a previously unknown essay by Hovell, entitled 'Rex Dei Gratia', recently came to light in the July 1915 issue (volume 7) of the Workers' Educational Association journal, *The Highway*.[10] This short essay, three and a half pages in length, has sat in plain sight since its publication, although there is no mention of it in Tout's biographical essay, nor has any reference been found in the Hovell papers held at the John Rylands Library. While the digitisation of *The Highway* has undoubtedly contributed to the rediscovery of this work, it should be noted that its authorship is misattributed in the ProQuest database: rather than being correctly attributed to Mark Hovell, the online listing identifies the author as a 'Mark Hoyell'. There is no question that the essay is by Hovell, however: it is signed by him, and the index to the issue also idenfies it as his contribution.

A Summary: 'Rex Dei Gratia'

'Rex Dei Gratia' offers a highly readable summary of some key details from John Neville Figgis's famous study, *The Divine Right of Kings*. First published in 1896 as part of the series of Cambridge Historical Essays, Figgis's book covered the historical and philosophical aspects of Divine Right theory, with a particular focus on sixteenth- and seventeenth-century English political thought. A second, expanded edition was published in 1914, and it was this edition that Hovell drew upon in his essay.[11] Hovell did not evaluate the merits of Figgis's book, but simply provided the reader with a precis of its main points:

> Mr Figgis says 'those who have exhausted their powers of satire in pouring scorn upon the theory [of divine right], have commonly been at little pains to understand it.' Let us see what our author has to tell us about it.[12]

Hovell's essay began by discussing the significance of 'D.G.' or 'Dei Gratia' ('by the Grace of God') on coins, and its relation to the concept of the Divine Right of Kings. From there, he led the reader to consider an important political question:

'on what grounds and by what sanction is one man permitted to exercise sovereign authority, even to the extent of depriving fellow men of their lives?'[13] Many would conclude that the ultimate justification for this power is the consent of the governed, but Hovell informed the reader that this perspective had emerged only two hundred years earlier; before that, authority was often justified by religious sanctions, implying a divine or moral order to which humans were bound. Here lay the ancient belief in kingship as divinely ordained, with kings viewed as the earthly representatives and descendants of gods. This concept evolved with the advent of Christianity: Christ was the sole Son of God, and earthly rulers were subject to His authority, altering the traditional notion of Divine Right of Kings.

From here, Hovell's account moved swiftly to consider the profound impact of Divine Right theory in shaping the political history of Europe. The reader was presented with brief coverage of the influence of the Church in Western Europe from the fifth to the fifteenth centuries, and of how political ideas were shaped by the Church: 'political ideas were formed in the mould of the Church Catholic and Universal, so there grew the idea of uniting all Christian men into one great political and religious society'.[14] This was followed by remarks on the Reformation and the impact of the rise of national consciousness, especially in England and France, in seeking to reject the Pope's authority. This national consciousness involved a sense of patriotism and unity among a group of people sharing common blood, culture and government, with distinct interests and destinies:

> It was a feeling of local self-sufficiency which grew up. In England and France events had caused this feeling to be concentrated upon the person and office of the King. In both countries the King it was who had triumphed over foreign foes, who had from time to time defined the Pope and all his Cardinals, and who had rescued the State from the horrors of civil war. In truth it was said that 'the King is the new Messiah.' To the King, therefore, men looked for deliverance from the bonds of Rome.[15]

Nevertheless, Hovell noted, doubts arose about the justifications for overthrowing the long-held belief in the Pope's Divine Right ('the thousand year old belief that the Pope ruled the souls of men by Right Divine as the Vicar of Christ').[16] A possible solution was to question the genuineness of the Pope's Divine Right and to propose instead that it was the King who held the Divine Right: 'men put forward a belief that the King's title was sanctioned by God as the basis for an attack upon the Pope's title. Here is the first justification for a belief in the Divine Right of Kings.'[17] But why was the concept of Divine Right invoked at all? The reason was to be found in the mindset of the period, and specifically, the prevailing ecclesiastical attitudes of the time, for 'the Bible was still the source of all knowledge and philosophy'.[18] From this developed the widely held belief that the King's sovereign power was delegated to him by God.

The Divine Right of the Pope was not the only challenge to the King; significant attacks also came from beliefs in the Divine Right of the Presbytery and the Divine Right of the People: 'the first was the belief of the Calvinists, the second of the

Jesuits, the latest and most able champions of Roman Catholicism'.[19] Where Calvinism promoted strict control over doctrine and morals ('in the belief in the absolute authority of the Church over the State it out-poped the Pope'),[20] the Jesuits opposed the King's claims by proposing a theory that eventually challenged the Divine Right of Kings ('the theory that society is founded on a compact between sovereign and people and that the people has a right to the resist or reject the King who violates the compact').[21] This theory, later developed by Hobbes, Locke and Rousseau, was more explosive in practice than the Divine Right doctrine.

The theory's final stage, articulated by Sir Robert Filmer during the reign of Charles II, abandoned justification for the Divine Right of Kings based on scriptural arguments, instead proposing that monarchy was natural due to the family being the fundamental societal unit. The argument here was that Divine Right was grounded in the idea that kingship was itself sanctioned by God: 'what was natural to mankind was clearly sanctioned by God who was the author of Man and Nature. Therefore as Kingship is natural, it is divinely sanctioned.'[22] As Hovell noted, however, this view could justify any form of governance as natural and divinely sanctioned. Reason, liberty and utility were also considered natural, providing as strong a basis for a state as monarchy. The theory of Natural Rights was therefore an indirect outcome of the theory of the Divine Right of Kings. Over these three and a half pages, Hovell had sketched out the history of the idea that monarchs held absolute authority by divine sanction. His overall summary was succinct:

> Such is the origin, growth and decay of this theory. It grew out a quarrel between Church and State: it became a means whereby the State threw off the control of ecclesiastics and presbyters: was maintained as a vindication of the unity and sovereignty of the Nation. It served these purposes and died away when its task was done.[23]

Context, Comments and Speculations

Given the known details of Hovell's life and work, the 'Rex Dei Gratia' presents something of a mystery. Even allowing for the breadth of Hovell's range of interests and teaching, the subject of the Divine Right of Kings can be seen as an unusual one for him to have published on in the Workers' Educational Association's journal. The Workers' Educational Association (WEA) had been founded in the early twentieth century by Albert and Frances Mansbridge, with the explicit goal of challenging the class-based restrictions of traditional learning by providing educational opportunities for the working classes.[24] It is evident that Hovell had been a popular tutor for the WEA, delivering tutorial classes on a variety of historical topics and periods: Modern History and Industrial History (delivered during the academic year 1910–11),[25] Modern History (1911–12),[26] Modern English History, 1750–1900 (1913–14),[27] and European History (1914–15).[28] At the outbreak of the First World War, Hovell and Professor Ramsey Muir (also from the University of Manchester) delivered a series of lectures organised by the Manchester Branch and the North-Western District Council of the WEA. These lectures covered the historical background and causes of the conflict, and regularly drew crowds of several hundred.[29] In addition to this, in 1914 and 1915, Hovell delivered one-off WEA talks on the history of trades unionism in the nineteenth century,[30] and the French Revolution.[31] Yet it seems highly unlikely that Figgis's study of divine right theory would have formed part of Hovell's various WEA courses on English and European History. Finally, we should note that Figgis's book does not connect to Hovell's study of Chartism: *The Divine Right of Kings* is not included in either the text or the bibliography of *The Chartist Movement*.

The WEA's journal, *The Highway* (subtitled 'A Monthly Journal of Education for the People), was launched in 1908 and provided a platform through which 'those engaged on manual labour may meet with those engaged in the profession of teaching to discuss the problems of education, and more particularly those problems which concern the workers'.[32] Although not connected with any of his WEA classes, the subject matter for Hovell's 1915 essay does not appear particularly unusual when compared with other materials published in *The Highway* at around that time. Numerous short reviews, summaries and commentaries, written by a variety of WEA tutors, can easily be identified, and these often focused on contemporary economic and social topics. These included Beveridge's 1909 book, *Unemployment: A Problem of Industry*;[33] Jackson's 1911 study of the progress of industrial cooperation in Bristol;[34] various works on agricultural and industrial history;[35] Layton's investigation into the impact of inflation on different sections of the community;[36] and even social commentaries such as Robert Tressell's 1914 book, *The Ragged Trousered Philanthropists*.[37] Mention should also be made of various reviews and essays on topics including economic history, political history and constitutional history, such as Arnold Toynbee's study of the Industrial Revolution,[38] Hilaire Belloc's study of the French Revolution,[39] the history of warfare in England,[40] J. H. B. Masterman's history of the British constitution,[41] and G. M. Trevelyan's *Garibaldi and the Making of Italy*.[42]

Figgis's book had also been promoted to *Highway* readers for some years as a key reading in the history of political philosophy. In 1910, Masterman published twelve short essays in *The Highway* detailing the history of the English people from Anglo-Saxon England through to the end of the nineteenth century. Two of these essays – the fifth and seventh, respectively 'The Birth of Modern England' and 'Puritan England, 1603–60' – made specific reference to the developing ideas of 'Divine right', and interested readers were directed to consult two key texts on political theory: Gooch's *English Democratic Ideas in the Seventeenth Century*, and Figgis's *The Theory of the Divine Right of Kings*.[43] It is also worth noting that two months after the publication of Hovell's essay, G. D. H. Cole produced a reading list on philosophical aspects of political theory in the Middle Ages, in which he strongly promoted Figgis's book.[44] Although an unusual subject matter for him, Hovell's essay therefore fits into this general class of short summaries and commentaries of books promoted to *Highway* readers.

The rediscovery of 'Rex Dei Gratia' also affords some opportunity for speculation, and I would like to briefly explore this by considering the contemporary context against which 'Rex Dei Gratia' was written. I would argue that it is possible to place the subject matter of Hovell's 1915 essay in the context of the contemporary political issues and debates that he was witnessing during the First World War.[45] The work's central theme – the Divine Right of Kings – can be located in wartime criticisms of the British government policy. An excellent example of this is the series of articles, entitled 'The War and Liberty', written by the liberal politician Herbert Samuel and published in the *New Statesman*, slightly later than Hovell's work, in 1917.[46] Focusing on the social and political impact of the war, Samuel warned explicitly that wartime mechanisms had eroded fundamental rights, thereby threatening the democratic fabric of society. The Defence of the Realm Act (DORA), passed in August 1914, had granted the British government unprecedented powers to intervene in the lives of British citizens in the name of national security and defence.[47] In setting out this argument, Samuel used historical examples to illustrate how wartime policies such as DORA operated as instruments of social control, diluting individual liberty and permitting the government to operate through administrative decree. Here he offered a specific critique, exemplified by the concept of the Divine Right of Kings. Wartime conditions and policies, he argued, had eroded democratic institutions and civil liberties, in a way that was reminiscent of the autocratic rule once justified by the Divine Right of Kings.[48]

Given the details set out in his 1915 essay, how might Hovell have reacted to these same issues? The limited scope of 'Rex Dei Gratia' does not permit us to draw any firm conclusions, so we must settle for speculation. Such speculation is nevertheless interesting, especially given Hovell's comments that belief in the Divine Right of Kings had been rooted in the political faith of those who saw it as a necessary means of maintaining the unity and sovereignty of the state against external threats:

> Belief in the Divine Right of Kings ... signified a passionate loyalty to the national monarch, which was essential in a time of violent change and external danger. If the practical application of the theory meant prosecution and restriction of individual freedom, men thought it a small price to pay for a strong and united front against foes.[49]

In other words, the potential of the monarch to limit individual freedom was accepted as a necessary trade-off for national strength. Shifting the focus and context to matters in Hovell's own time, might Hovell have drawn upon this historical analogy and also considered DORA as a necessary trade-off for national strength during wartime? Or, had he lived, might Hovell have followed the same path as critics such as Samuel, and promoted historical awareness (of the Divine Right of Kings) in an effort to safeguard democratic principles and individual freedoms against absolute (wartime) authority?

The discovery of 'Rex Dei Gratia' provides an opportunity for us to speculate as to Hovell's wider views on wartime politics. Such questions are interesting to consider, but the current evidence of Hovell's life and work provides no materials for supporting any clear answers. Instead, we must focus our attention on two key points. The first is to appreciate that Hovell's readable commentary on the Divine Right of Kings is now the only identified work published during his lifetime. The second, and I would argue the more important point, is to recognise how this 1915 work, short and basic though it may be, serves to enhance our appreciation of Hovell as a teacher and as a historian.

Notes

1. 'Manchester Grammar School', *Manchester Guardian* (14 July 1898), p. 5.
2. 'The University: A Conferment of Degrees', *Manchester Guardian* (5 July 1909), p. 5. Hovell's was the only first-class degree in history awarded in 1909, out of a total cohort of eight students.
3. 'University Intelligence', *Manchester Guardian* (10 June 1910), p. 9.
4. *Ibid.*
5. The announcements of Hovell's death can be found in 'The Casualties', *Manchester Guardian* (18 August 1916), p. 7; 'The Late Second Lieutenant Mark Hovell', *Manchester Guardian* (21 August 1916), p. 4; E. H. Jones, 'In Memoriam – Mark Hovell', *The Highway*, 9 (1916), 56–7.
6. T. F. Tout, 'Introduction', in Mark Hovell, *The Chartist Movement* (Manchester, 1918), pp. xxi–xxxvii.
7. The John Rylands Library also holds a useful file of newspaper cuttings covering details of Hovell's life, together with reviews of *The Chartist Movement*, complied by Hovell's widow between 1918 and 1925 (Manchester, John Rylands Library, Mark Hovell Papers, GB 133 HOV/3/2/2).
8. Chris Godden, 'Introduction: The Life and Legacy of Mark Hovell', *Bulletin of the John Rylands Library*, 94 (2018), 1–13.
9. Tout, 'Introduction', p. xxxiii. The collection of Hovell's personal papers, largely covering the years 1906–15 and preserved at the John Rylands Library, includes two unpublished essays. The first of these is Hovell's Bachelor of Arts dissertation from 1909, entitled 'Political Relations of England and Ireland in the Reign of Richard II', which, despite its potential interest, has yet to attract the attention of medieval scholars (Mark Hovell Papers HOV/1/1/10). The second is an undated manuscript lecture, entitled 'Mr Gladstone as a Tory', and very likely related to one or more of the university tutorial classes on modern history that Hovell delivered between 1910 and 1915 (Mark Hovell Papers, GB 133 HOV/1/1/27).
10. Mark Hovell, 'Rex Dei Gratia', *The Highway*, 7 (1915), 158–61.
11. John Neville Figgis, *The Divine Right of Kings*, 2nd edn (Cambridge, 1914). Figgis's book was itself an enlarged version of an essay first submitted for the Prince Consort Dissertation Prize in 1892. In addition to the original essay on the divine-right theory (the original text was left largely unchanged), the second edition included three new essays: 'Aaron's Rod Blossoming or Jus Divinum in 1646' (delivered as an address at the University of Leeds in 1913), 'Erastus and Erastianism' (first published in the

Journal of Theological Studies in 1900), and 'Bartolus and the Development of European Political Ideas' (first published in the *Transactions of the Royal Historical Society* in 1905).

12 Hovell, 'Rex Dei Gratia', 158.
13 *Ibid.*
14 *Ibid.*
15 Hovell, 'Rex Dei Gratia', 159.
16 *Ibid.*
17 *Ibid.*
18 *Ibid.*
19 Hovell, 'Rex Dei Gratia', 160.
20 *Ibid.*
21 *Ibid.*
22 Hovell, 'Rex Dei Gratia', 161.
23 *Ibid.*
24 Albert Mansbridge, 'The Beginning of the WEA', *The Highway*, 16 (1924), 132–8.
25 'University Tutorial Classes, 1910–1911', *The Highway*, 3 (1910), 29–30.
26 'University Tutorial Classes, 1911–1912', *The Highway*, 4 (1911), 27–9.
27 'University Tutorial Classes, 1913–1914', *The Highway*, 6 (1913), 27–9. A copy of the printed syllabus for this series of class lectures is preserved in the Hovell Papers in the John Rylands Library (GB 133 HOV/4/4).
28 'University Tutorial Classes, 1914–1915', *The Highway*, 7 (1914), 39–41. It is likely that this lecture series is related to material covering European history, *c.*1815–1910, held in the Hovell Papers (GB 133 HOV/1/1/21).
29 'The Finger Post: North Western District', *The Highway*, 7 (1914), 29–32, 48–50; 'Manchester and the War', *Manchester Guardian* (12 October 1914), p. 7; 'When France Was Beaten: The Story of 1870', *Manchester Guardian* (26 October 1914), p. 7; 'University Extension Lectures on the War', *Manchester Courier and Lancashire General Advertiser* (5 November 1914), p. 4.
30 'Lecture List: Lectures and Single Talks', *The Highway* – London Supplement, 6 (1914), 4.
31 'Education and the Club Movement', *The Highway*, 7 (1915), 84. This talk was delivered on 19 November 1914 at Radcliffe Trades Hall Club (GB 133 HOV/1/1/20).
32 'Our Aims and Objects', *The Highway*, 1 (1908), 1–2. A great deal of material published in the early years of *The Highway* centred around contemporary economics, social and political issues, economic history and industrial history.
33 S. J. Chapman, 'Review – Unemployment: A Problem of Industry', *The Highway*, 1 (1909), 121–2.
34 D. H. Macgregor, 'A Study in Democracy', *The Highway*, 3 (1911), 138–9.
35 S. J. Chapman, 'The Evolution of Industry', *The Highway*, 4 (1912), 93; H. Clay, 'A New Text Book on English Industrial History', *The Highway*, 4 (1912), 167; K. Leys, 'The Agrarian Problem in the 16th Century', *The Highway*, 5 (1912), 48–9.
36 M. Epstein, 'An Introduction to the Study of Prices', *The Highway*, 4 (1912), 122.
37 J. St George Heath, 'The Ragged Trousered Philanthropists', *The Highway*, 7 (1915), 110–11.

38 J. W. Mackail, 'Arnold Toynbee and the Industrial Revolution', *The Highway*, 1 (1908), 14.
39 A. J. Clark, 'The French Revolution', *The Highway*, 3 (1911), 151–2.
40 Kenneth Bell, 'Warfare in England', *The Highway*, 5 (1912), 6.
41 P. A. Brown, 'A Text Book for Tutorial Classes', *The Highway*, 4 (1912), 106–7.
42 Kenneth Bell, 'Garibaldi and the Making of Italy', *The Highway*, 4 (1912), 52–4.
43 J. H. B. Masterman, 'The History of the English People: V – The Birth-Time of Modern England', *The Highway*, 3 (1911), 74–5; J. H. B. Masterman, 'The History of the English People: VII – Puritan England, 1603–60', *The Highway*, 3 (1911), 104–5.
44 G. D. H. Cole, 'At the Sign of the Book', *The Highway*, 7 (1915), 205–7.
45 Once again, Tout's biographical essay is the only evidence of Hovell's attitudes towards the war: '[Hovell] had a stern sense of obligation and a keen eye for realities ... he fully realised the inevitableness of the struggle, and he knew that every man was bound to take his place in the grave and prolonged effort by which alone England could escape overwhelming disaster': Tout, 'Introduction', pp. xxxiii– xxxiv.
46 See, Herbert Samuel, 'War and Liberty – I: Constitutional Liberty', *The New Statesman* (26 May 1917), pp. 174–6; Herbert Samuel, 'War and Liberty – II: National Liberty, *The New Statesman* (2 June 1917), pp. 200–2; Herbert Samuel, 'The War and Liberty – III: Liberty of Speech and of the Press', *The New Statesman* (9 June 1917), pp. 223–5; Herbert Samuel, 'The War and Liberty – IV: Personal Liberty', *The New Statesman* (16 June 2017), pp. 246–8; Herbert Samuel, 'The War and Liberty – V: Industrial Liberty', *The New Statesman* (23 June 1917), pp. 272–4; Herbert Samuel, 'The War and Liberty – VI: Conclusion', *The New Statesman* (30 June 1917), p. 297. Samuel was not the only wartime critic of government legislation; another interesting set of articles on the same theme was published by the economic and political commentator J. A Hobson in *The Nation and Atheneum* in 1916. See J. A. Hobson, 'The War and British Liberties – I: The Suppression of Free Speech', *The Nation and Atheneum* (15 April 1916), pp. 68–9; J. A. Hobson, 'The War and British Liberties – II: Secret Trial or No Trial', *The Nation and Atheneum* (29 April 1916), pp. 123–5; J. A. Hobson, 'The War and British Liberties – III: The Claims of the State upon the Individual', *The Nation and Atheneum* (10 June 1916), pp. 307–8; J. A. Hobson, 'The War and British Liberties – IV. Liberty and a True War Economy', *The Nation and Atheneum* (29 July 1916), pp. 524–5.
47 For an excellent summary of wartime legislation, see G. R. Rubin, 'The Defence of the Realm Act and Other Emergency Laws', in Hew Strachan (ed.), *The British Home Front and the First World War* (Cambridge: Cambridge University Press, 2023), pp. 78–94.
48 Herbert Samuel, 'War and Liberty – I: Constitutional Liberty', *The New Statesman* (26 May 1917), pp. 174–6.
49 Hovell, 'Rex Dei Gratia', 160.

EU authorised representative for GPSR:
Easy Access System Europe, Mustamäe tee 50,
10621 Tallinn, Estonia
gpsr.requests@easproject.com

www.ingramcontent.com/pod-product-compliance
Ingram Content Group UK Ltd.
Pitfield, Milton Keynes, MK11 3LW, UK
UKHW051848210426